DATE DUE		
APR 2 9		
MAY 3 1		
muraoka		

D.Beem

MEXICO

Giant of the South

by Eileen Latell Smith

Dillon Press, Inc. Minneapolis, Minnesota 55415

Library of Congress Cataloging in Publication Data

Smith, Eileen Latell.
  Mexico, giant of the south.

  (Discovering our heritage)
  Bibliography: p. 155.
  Includes index.
  1. Mexico—Juvenile literature.   I. Title.
F1208.5.S63   1983   972   83-7334
ISBN 0-87518-242-9

Dillon Press, Inc., 500 South Third Street
Minneapolis, Minnesota 55415

Printed in the United States of America
          4 5 6 7 8 9 10 91 90 89 88 87 86 85

The photographs are reproduced through the courtesy of the American Broadcasting Company; the Greater San Antonio Chamber of Commerce; the Mexican National Tourist Council; Mission San Juan Capistrano; the Secretaría de Educación Pública of Mexico; Denzil Smith; and Shelley Williams.

Contents

Fast Facts About Mexico

Official Name: Estados Unidos Mexicanos ("United
  Mexican States")
Capital: Mexico City
Location: Latin America; Mexico is the northern-
  most country in Latin America and shares a two-
  thousand-mile border with the United States
  stretching from Texas to California.
Area: 758,136 square miles (1,963,564 square
  kilometers); the greatest distances in Mexico are
  1,250 miles (2,012 kilometers) from north to
  south and 1,900 miles (3,060 kilometers) from
  east to west. Mexico has 6,320 miles (10,170
  kilometers) of coastline.
Elevation: *Highest*—Orizaba (Citlaltépetl), 18,701
  feet (5,700 meters) above sea level. *Lowest*—a
  point near Mexicali 33 feet (10 meters) below sea
  level.
Population: *Estimated 1983 Population*—74,507,000.
  Distribution—67 percent of the people live in or
  near cities; 33 percent live in rural areas.
  Density—98 persons per square mile (38 persons
  per square kilometer).
Form of Government: Republic; *Head of Government*—president.

Important Products: Beans, coffee, corn, cotton, fruits, sugar cane, wheat; cement, chemicals, clothing, fertilizers, iron and steel, iron ore, natural gas, petroleum, silver, tin, zinc.

Basic Unit of Money: Peso.

Major Languages: Spanish and major Indian languages—Maya, Mixtec, Náhuatl, Otomí, Tarascan, and Zapotec.

Major Religion: Nearly all Mexicans belong to the Roman Catholic church.

Flag: Three broad, vertical stripes of green, white, and red with the coat of arms—an eagle perched on a cactus and clutching a snake—in the center, a white stripe.

National Anthem: "Himno Nacional de México" ("National Anthem of Mexico")

Major Holidays: Carnival season—January 17 through the beginning of Lent; Easter Day; Independence Day—September 16; Guadalupe Day—December 12; Las Posadas—December 16-24; Christmas Day—December 25.

1. *Giant of the South*

Mexico today is like a giant with one foot in the past, and one foot in the present, who with both hands reaches out to the future. Giant pyramids and ruins of ancient cities more than two thousand years old still stand as signs of a proud past. Everywhere are beautiful Spanish-style churches, many of them built soon after Columbus sailed to America. In the cities skyscrapers tower silently, while modern supermarkets and superhighways bustle below. They are part of the present. Huge pumping units pull oil from big pools deep in the earth. Factories hum. They are working for the future.

Modern-day Mexico shares a two-thousand-mile border with the southwestern United States—California, Arizona, New Mexico, and Texas. The border is a busy place. Every day trucks full of fruit, vegetables, and meat rumble across from Mexico on their way to American cities. All kinds of goods pour across the border from the factories of Mexico's northeast near Texas. Mexican farm workers cross over each year to harvest the crops of U.S. farms, and city people fly up to U.S. border towns to buy American television sets, appliances, and clothing.

On weekends, especially, Mexican towns near the border are full of Americans. Colorful open-air markets overflow with handmade leather sandals and purses, glass, jewelry, baskets, toys, and pottery. Mexicans like to make these things with their hands,

Open-air markets like this one are a common sight in Mexican towns near the U.S. border.

and many Americans come to the border towns to buy them.

Border towns are typical in the far north of Mexico, but they make up only one small part of a big country. Four Mexicos could fit into the area of the United States. Yet Mexico is three times as large as Spain or France, and eight times as large as England.

If you were to take a map and draw a line around the outside edges of Mexico, it would look, roughly, like a triangle. It is very wide at the top where it joins the United States. Then it gets thinner at the bottom where it curves to the east and connects with Central America. Within this large country—a democratic republic called *Estados Unidos Mexicanos* ("United Mexican States")—are thirty-one states and the federal district of Mexico City.

Water lies on both sides of Mexico. In the west, the Pacific surf beats against jagged cliffs and rolls into wide, sandy beaches. Along the northwest coast, in Baja California ("Lower California"), many fisheries thrive. Shrimp boats cut through the blue waters, and pearl divers plunge into the depths.

Farther down the coast, the beach bends into a huge horseshoe-shaped bay. Terraced hotels overlook the bright, blue waters of Acapulco, speckled with the white sails of boats. Out in the deep sea, dolphins, whales, and furry seals play.

Sailboats glide swiftly through the bright blue ocean waters near Acapulco.

On the east coast the warm waters of the Gulf of Mexico lap the shore. The land along this coast is flat and low, with marshes and shady lagoons where alligators and crocodiles lurk in the shadows. Heat and humidity swell the air. No wonder Mexicans call this area the *tierra caliente*, or hotlands.

The gulf coast glistens with sparkling beaches. Suntanned children splash and swim in the gentle waves, while the more daring dive off rocks close to shore. But none swim out very far, for they know that fierce, hungry sharks glide unseen beneath the surface. Scientists called marine biologists come here

A view from a hotel balcony overlooking Acapulco's horseshoe-shaped bay.

from all over the world to study the sea life.

The southeastern end of Mexico is where Spanish explorers first sailed hundreds of years ago. As Grijalva rounded the tip of the Yucatán peninsula, he saw ancient cities and temples. A proud and powerful Indian people, the Mayas, lived there long ago. Then, suddenly, most of the Mayas left their cities. No one knows why. Grijalva found only a few scattered tribes and the ruins of once great cities, overgrown with heavy vines and jungle plants.

In Chiapas, the southernmost state of Mexico, tropical rains douse Tabasco almost every day of the year. Mexicans say that it is the wettest place in the world. Chameleons hide in the jungle trees where they take on the color of the bark or leaves for camouflage. Parrots chatter, and monkeys jabber. Iguanas dart about, tongues flicking, looking like tiny dinosaurs.

About an hour's drive inland from the gulf coast, the land begins to rise quickly into rugged mountains. First there are forests of oaks, and then as the land soars higher, firs and pine. Bears, jaguars, and pumas still prowl in these wild highlands. The taller peaks are capped with snow that never melts.

Mountains, called the *Sierra Madre*, cover much of Mexico. One range of peaks rises in the east and another in the west. The two ranges come together in the south, forming the shape of a giant *V*.

Tiny villages are nestled into valleys in the mountains. Some can be reached only by footpaths. Children who live near these towns ride horses, donkeys, or, more often, burros. Since the stubborn burros usually want to go their own way, country children are used to walking a long way to school.

Rising high in the Sierra Madre is the third tallest mountain in all of North America. Once an active volcano, Orizaba looms more than three and a half miles (5,700 meters) high. Nearby rise a number of other old volcanoes, no longer active, with peaks almost as tall as Orizaba.

From time to time, new volcanoes appear in Mexico, too. One day in 1943, two brothers who lived near the tiny village of Paricutín watched as the ground around a hole in their cornfield cracked and swelled. Gray ash and sulfur gases exploded thousands of feet up into the air. For months the swollen mound grew and grew until it formed a cinder cone a thousand feet high.

Villagers fled as the thick ash filled the air. Roofs collapsed under piles of heavy ash, and houses crumbled. When lava began to flow, the little village was covered, as well as San Juan, a neighboring town. Paricutín, named after the tiny village it first covered, erupted from time to time for nine years before it lay still.

Away from the volcanoes, high up between the two ranges of the Sierra Madre, is a very large, flat area called the Plateau of Mexico. The northern part of this plateau is desert, dry and dusty. Rain falls on its cacti and scrub trees only three or four days a year. Towns are few and far between. In the noonday sun, rattlesnakes and lizards doze in the shade of rocks, while at night the howls of coyotes pierce the air.

Most of Mexico's largest cities are found in the southern part of the great plateau. Guadalajara, with its broad, tree-lined streets, and the colonial cities of Guanajuato and Morelia rise there. León, Querétaro,

San Luis Potosí, and others are all connected by highways and railways. Mexico City, the capital, lies where the two ranges of the Sierra Madre come together to form a single row of tall peaks. Several of these are also old volcanoes.

From the capital, two high mountains loom to the south and east. One is named Popocatépetl, or "Popo" for short. The other is called Iztaccíhuatl, or "the sleeping woman." Mexicans say that its outline against the sky looks like a woman lying on her side.

Sprawling below the mountains is one of the largest cities in the world. Trolleys, cars, and buses jam the streets. Horns honk and cab drivers yell at each other. The metro, or subway, rumbles underground while airplanes zoom overhead. Sidewalks are filled with office workers hurrying to skyscrapers of glass and steel. Through the crowds country women move gracefully, balancing bundles on their heads.

Mexico City is also one of the world's fastest growing cities. Skeletons of new buildings rise up everywhere, as workers busily dig out places for still more. Many workers tote dirt in baskets which hang on their heads from straps around their foreheads. They can carry more that way than with a wheelbarrow.

Each year thousands of villagers move to the big

Walking in the city, a strong Mexican woman balances a large basket on her head while she carries another one in her arms.

The Independence Monument rises gracefully in the heart of Mexico City.

city in search of work. Whole families pile into buses or trains carrying chickens, parrots, and all of their belongings tied up in cartons. Often they move in with relatives. Many of these newcomers can neither read nor write and have never used a telephone or subway. For them city life is a big surprise.

Dodging traffic, city children play in the streets. Boys kick soccer balls and swing baseball bats. Girls jump rope and play tag on the sidewalks. Some young people live in houses or apartments that look a lot like American ones. Inside are refrigerators, electric ranges, washing machines, and television sets. These Mexican children watch many of the same TV programs as American kids do, but, of course, in Spanish.

Other children aren't so lucky. They live in crowded, tiny shacks made of wood or even cardboard, with tin roofs. Many have no running water or electricity. Little boys sell chewing gum and shine shoes to earn money so that their families can have enough food to eat.

Many Mexican families, rich and poor, have pet dogs. A favorite is the little chihuahua. Chihuahuas have almost no hair, pointed ears, and large, round eyes. Since they shiver and shake and always seem to be cold, their owners make tiny coats for them to wear.

The chihuahuas may look cold, but the weather is really springlike all year round in the central plateau. That high up, 4,000 feet (1,200 meters) to 9,000 feet (2,700 meters) above sea level, it never gets very hot. And yet, because the sun is so warm, it never gets very cold, either.

If you lived on the plateau, you would never need a heavy coat, earmuffs, or wool gloves. But from May to October, you would get wet without an umbrella, for showers fall every afternoon. Then, during the rest of the year, it is dry and sunny. There are only two seasons in Mexico, the rainy season and the dry season.

Since most of Mexico lacks good rainfall, water must be used carefully. Mexicans have built dams in rivers to save water and make electricity. Some of the water is used to irrigate fields, while the rest flows into houses in cities.

Many small villages have no running water at all, only a well in the main square. Every day villagers meet at the well and chat as they draw water. Barefoot children carry big earthen jars of water back to their houses. Women and girls walk to nearby creeks to wash clothes on the rocks.

Water is so precious in Mexico that Mexicans are careful never to waste any. Even dirty dishwater is recycled—Mexicans use it to water the flowers!

In the upper part of Yucatán, there is no water at all on the surface of the land. But deep underground, rivers run, and in some places great pits have formed. Scientists call them sinkholes, which are places where the thin layer of limestone soil caved in and settled to the underground water level. Long ago, Indians built wooden steps down to the water. Even today, voices and laughter echo from deep in the earth when families go down to get water for cooking and washing.

Mexico has few lakes. The largest is Lake Chapala, near Guadalajara. Fishing villages and vacation homes line the shores of Lake Pátzcuaro, where families go swimming and boating. Many families go to one of the lakes for the weekend to relax after a week in the busy city.

The great salt lake, Texcoco, once stretched across nine miles (fifteen kilometers) where Mexico

On Lake Pátzcuaro, a Mexican Indian fishes in much the same way that his ancestors did centuries ago.

City stands today. The palaces and pyramids of the Aztec capital, Tenochtitlán, rose up on a nearby marshy island in the shallow lake. Three earth-filled roads, or causeways, connected it to the lakeshore.

Slowly, over the years, many of the heavy pyramids and palaces sank into the marsh. Then, when the Spaniards came, they built churches and buildings right on top of them. Today, these buildings are sinking, too—some as much as a foot each year. Only a small part of the lake remains on the edge of a suburb of the modern capital.

Nearby Mexico City lies Lake Xochimilco, which means "place of the field of flowers" in the Aztec language. Once Aztec farmers tended plots of vegetables which floated on woven frames in the shallow water. Flowers still grow, and every Sunday people flock to the lake to admire them. Families and lovers, young and old, ride and picnic in flat-bottomed boats pushed along with poles. In some of the hidden, quiet spots, farmers still grow vegetables and spices just the way the Aztecs did hundreds of years ago.

Water is important in the mountains, too, where narrow, flat terraces are carved into the steep slopes for farming. Early each morning, men and boys head into the fields. During planting time, older children help by poking holes in the ground with pointed sticks and planting the seeds, while younger children fill in the holes and stamp on the ground. The dependable rains and sunshine make the crops grow well.

Though water is scarce in Mexico, valuable minerals are not. Mexico has rich deposits of silver, gold, copper, coal, lead, zinc, sulfur, and oil. Old mining towns with cobblestone streets still thrive, such as Taxco on the road from Mexico City to Acapulco. A few others turned into dusty ghost towns when the silver or gold ran out.

Several years ago, new oil discoveries along the east coast caused a lot of excitement. Within a few years, Mexico became a major oil-producing nation. Today, enough oil is produced to meet all its own needs and to sell much more to other countries. Recently, though, the price of oil has fallen because of a worldwide economic downturn. Because Mexico depends on oil sales to help its own economy grow, the drop in oil prices has caused hard times for its people.

While Mexico grows and moves into the age of industry, reminders of the past are everywhere. Many thick-walled Spanish mansions with cool central patios are now restaurants and inns for all to enjoy. Richly carved churches grace the center of every town. One city, Puebla, is said to have more than one thousand churches. A church or chapel was built on top of every Indian temple and pyramid.

In Mexico City, new pieces of the Aztec past appear every day. While digging for the metro, workers' shovels uncovered beads, bowls, canoes, and even a little pyramid. The pyramid is now part of a subway station. In 1978 a worker's ax clanged into a hard object. It turned out to be a part of the Great Temple of the Aztecs, just a stone's throw from the National Palace where the president and other top officials work.

The old stands proudly next to the new. As families carry drinking water in jugs from ancient water holes, oil wells pump many thousands of barrels of oil a day. Some children ride to school on burros, while other travelers fly on jets. Mexico has woven together bits of its proud past into a colorful new blend. Today it stands once more as the giant of the south.

2. Of Mexican Ways

Most Mexicans have dark hair, flashing black eyes, and golden skin. Yet some look like their Indian ancestors, with high cheekbones, almond-shaped eyes, and shiny, blue-black hair. Others, especially in the cities, are fair-skinned, blue-eyed people with light hair and European features. They are all Mexicans.

The ancestors of most Mexicans can be traced back to the time when Spanish explorers invaded the Aztec empire. When Cortés conquered the Aztecs in 1519, there were 182 Indian tribes in what is now Mexico. He and his men married Indian women, and their children were the first *mestizos*, or people of mixed Indian and white ancestry. As more Spaniards landed, there was more mixing, so that today most Mexicans are mestizos.

Now Mexicans are proud to be mestizos, but in the past they were taught to be ashamed of their Indian ancestors. For a long time Mexico was called New Spain. Only Spaniards could rule, and they owned much of the land. Most mestizos and Indians were very poor.

At last writers and artists began to tell of the

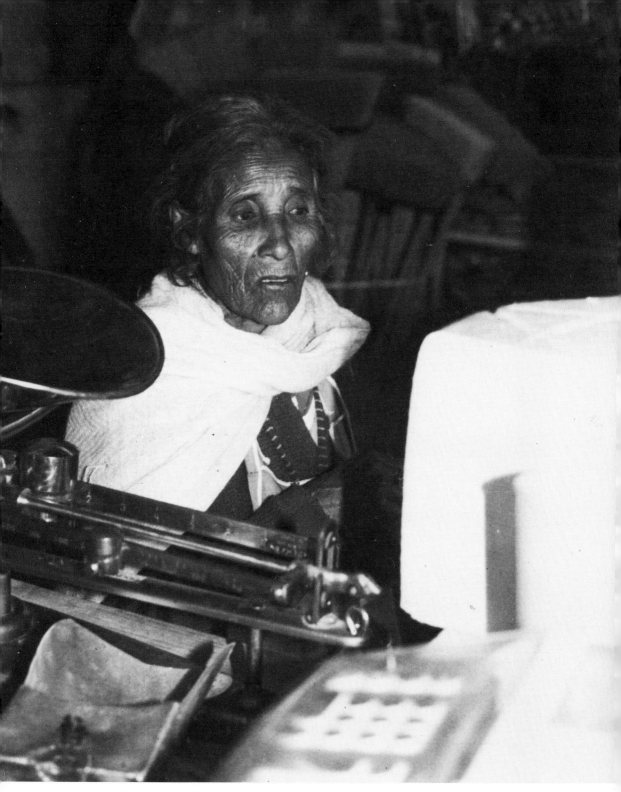

Like this woman, most Mexicans are mestizos, *people of mixed Spanish and Indian ancestry.*

problems of the poor peasants, the *campesinos.* One famous book, *Los de Abajo* (The Underdogs), by a man named Azuela, showed their struggle. People began to learn about the great cities and proud ways of the Indians. Today, when a Mexican boasts of his European ancestors, his friends will tell him, "Don't be so Spanish!"

Not only are there different types of people in Mexico, they dress in all sorts of ways. City businessmen wear suits and fine leather shoes. Their wives have their hair cut in the latest styles and buy fashions from Paris and New York. Workers in coveralls dig ditches. Taxi drivers in sunglasses and brightly colored shirts speed through narrow streets. Widows dress all in black and cover their heads with scarves. Delivery boys in worn pants and jackets ride bicycles while balancing baskets on their heads. Beggars in rags hold out their hands for a few pesos.

In the countryside campesinos wear white pajamalike suits, often pulled in at the ankle and tied about the waist with a cord. Old tires cut into sandals called *huaraches* are strapped onto their feet with leather thongs. Indian women and girls prefer long full skirts and embroidered blouses. They braid their hair with bits of wool or ribbon and often pile it on top of their heads.

Many times Mexicans can tell what region a man

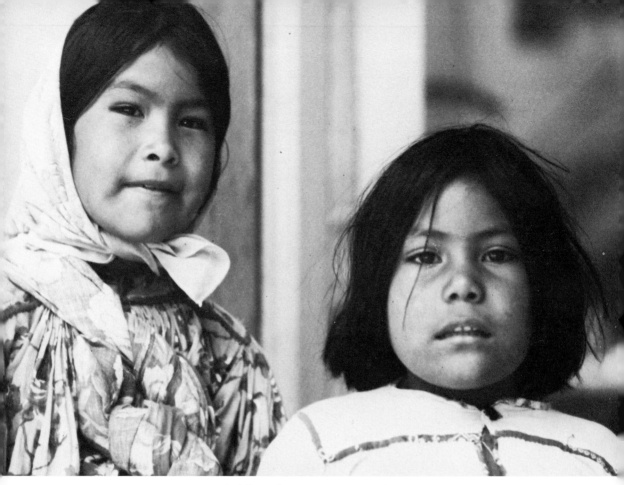

These handsome children live in Mexico City.

comes from just by his hat. Men from Michoacán sport hats with low crowns and dangling ribbons. In Veracruz men like hats with high, round crowns. *Charros*, or horsemen, from Jalisco wear wide-brimmed, felt hats, trimmed with silver and gold braid.

Mexicans know where a woman is from by the way she wraps her shawl, the *rebozo*. Covering the head, pulled tightly around the neck, or draped loosely about the shoulders—all these ways show that a woman is from a particular part of the country. In fact, for many women rebozos come in handy for lots of things. At the marketplace they double as shopping bags. Tiny babies cuddle up and nap like papooses in their rebozos.

There are also many differences in the way Mexicans live. Almost half of them still live in the country. Since most country homes have no electricity, people often go to bed early and rise with the crows of roosters. Simple meals are cooked over small fireplaces in the corners of one- or two-room huts made of sticks and mud or rocks. With no chimneys, smoke drifts out the open windows and up through roofs of tin, straw, or tiles.

City life is like another world. Some wealthy Mexicans iive in large, modern houses inside high walls with big iron gates. There are also many small, older, Spanish-style homes built around central patios. Other families live in huge government housing projects in one- or two-bedroom apartments. The poorest families fill the slums in shacks much like the huts in the countryside.

While there are great differences in the way Mexicans dress and live, more important are the bonds that make them one people. For one thing, almost all Mexicans speak Spanish. Before the missionaries taught the Indians Spanish, the Indian peoples could not talk to one another because each spoke a different language.

Even today, many Indians still speak *Náhuatl*, the language of the Aztecs. In fact, we speak a little ourselves. *Chocolate* and *tomato*, words we use every day, come from Náhuatl. Other Indians may speak Maya or Otomí, but most of them learn Spanish, too.

Nearly all Mexicans also share the experience of a strong family life. Most families are large; many parents have ten or more children! On Sundays and holidays, families usually visit other relatives. A crowd gathers with everyone laughing, chatting, and hugging each other.

From the time they are very small, children play a part in these family events. In such big families there is always a baptism, wedding, or birthday, and all the children take part in the celebrations. In this way they learn how to behave well with people of all ages. Children are taught to be polite, too. They show respect for their elders and obey their parents.

Men are the heads of families in Mexico, and business and politics are for men only. This strong sense of male pride is called *machismo*. A man will never wash dishes or cook. He wants his wife to stay home to care for the children and entertain friends. As soon as he earns enough money, he will hire a

A mother shares a happy moment with her daughters.

maid to help her take care of the house. And whenever he can, he will help relatives of the family, too.

Often parents, children, grandparents, and perhaps an uncle or even a cousin live under the same roof. Because of this living arrangement, children have many people to love and take care of them. Mexicans don't even have a word for "babysitter" since they rarely have a need for one with so many relatives around. Family members will take care of a child for love, not money.

In Mexico, "family" also includes distant cousins and relatives. Even godparents are considered family. Many Mexicans can travel all around Mexico and never stay at a hotel. They just stop by and visit their relatives!

Families not only live together and visit a lot, they also work together. In some little towns, all the officials are related, and the businesspeople may be, too. When a new worker is needed, it's not unusual to hire a cousin.

With all this togetherness, the worst kind of insult in Mexico is to say something nasty about someone's family—especially a mother or a sister. These are fighting words, for any Mexican will defend the family's honor. That loyalty comes before anything else.

Friendliness is another part of being Mexican. Almost all Mexicans, and especially the people from Oaxaca, will welcome strangers into their homes. From the poorest villager to the wealthiest businessman, warmth and kindness are offered to all.

Whether at home or out with friends, Mexicans are seldom afraid to show their feelings. They laugh heartily when they are happy and cry openly when they are sad. Men hug each other with a firm *abrazo* and a slap on the back. Women kiss each other on

These fun-loving students worked together to stage a school play.

each cheek when they greet and depart. Friends walk arm in arm down the street. Parents hug and fuss over their children. In all parts of their daily lives, Mexicans like to touch those they know and like.

Like the family, religion touches almost everyone's life in Mexico. Nearly all Mexicans belong to the Roman Catholic church. The Virgin of Guadalupe is thought of as the spiritual mother of the country, and each town has a patron saint. The saint's birthday is the most important fiesta of the year. People dress up statues of the saint and celebrate with parades, music, dancing, and fireworks.

During the big fiestas, some Indians in the remote countryside don costumes of leopards and tigers and

Spanish *conquistadores*. They dance nonstop in the churches for days. All the men take turns as they play out the arrival of Cortés in Mexico and his meeting with the Aztecs. This is their way of celebrating their saint's day.

Most Mexicans give saints' names to their children. Since María is the most popular name for girls, each year millions of girls named María celebrate their saint's day. For Mexicans, saints' days are more important than birthdays.

Whether it's fiesta time, or anytime, the pace of life in Mexico is slower than life in the United States. People stop at outdoor cafés and relax and chat with friends. Mexicans don't like to check their watches or hurry to be somewhere on time.

Imagine what it would be like to get together with some friends after school. If you agreed to meet them at three o'clock, you wouldn't expect your friends to show up until half-past three or maybe even four. You would think of time much differently from the way you think of it now.

Every day in Mexico, life slows down at *siesta* time. We often use the Spanish word *siesta* to mean a short nap. Actually, it comes from the latin *sexta*, which means the sixth hour. The idea behind it is that the first six hours of the day are for working, and the rest are for living. In Mexico that is the way of life.

Many offices and shops close for two hours in the afternoon. Everyone who can goes home to eat a big meal, relax, and be with family.

Even at work, Mexicans want to take pleasure in what they do, and many of them enjoy working with their hands. In the mountain town of Taxco, silver is bent, pounded, and shaped into fancy ornaments and beautiful designs of many shapes and sizes. The weavers of Oaxaca are famous the world over for their hand-loomed tapestries. In the tiniest shack, the click-clack of a sewing machine run by pushing on a foot peddle is a common sound. Even small girls learn to embroider and sew.

No matter what their work, Mexicans share the central plaza of cities and towns for early evening band concerts on Sundays. Wealthy or poor, young or old, whole families walk together, arm in arm.

In some small towns, there is still a *paseo* where many young people first meet. Groups of girls stroll slowly around the plaza, while young men and boys walk along in the opposite direction. The young men admire the girls, who pretend not to notice. Sometimes the boys make flattering remarks called *piropos* to the girls, who act as if they didn't hear. Parents and relatives sit along the side, watching the young people and chatting and listening to the music.

Young people usually prefer to meet in groups

where they can dance and sing together. American rock music is popular, but Mexican ballads and love songs are still the favorites. Often the same song will be popular for many years, for Mexicans are loyal to their singers, too.

The most lively music is from Guadalajara in the state of Jalisco, which Mexicans call the cradle of

In Guadalajara a mariachi *band plays a lively tune.*

A carriage stands waiting to ride through the romantic city of Guadalajara.

poets and romance. They can barely say "Guadalajara" without a deep sigh of longing. People from this romantic city are called *tapatíos*. To a Mexican this word means simply "happy and gay."

Jalisco is also the home of the *mariachi*, who wear *charro* hats and black suits with short, braid-trimmed jackets. Carrying violins, guitars, and horns, these street bands stroll along and play catchy tunes for people in sidewalk cafés.

Jalisco isn't the only area of Mexico known for its

music. In the east coast city of Veracruz, small boys entertain people on the streets with the soft, gentle sounds of the *marimba*. And all over the country, popular folk songs known as *corridos* tell stories about the heroes of the Mexican Revolution or the bandits who robbed from the rich to give to the poor.

Dances are just as important to Mexicans as their music. In fact, each region of Mexico has its own colorful folk dances. In the plume dance from Oaxaca, dancers leap about in helmets topped by bright feathers. In the Yaqui deer dance from Sonora, dancers dress like deer, with antlers and ankle bells. Heels tap and skirts swirl in the *jarabe tapatío*, which we call the Mexican hat dance. And once a year in the town of Cholula, dancers twirl on top of the world's highest pyramid. Music for these high-flying dancers is played on armadillo shells, gourds, and wooden boxes. To see many of these dances performed, Mexicans go to the Palace of Fine Arts in Mexico City and watch the Ballet Folklórico, a world famous dance company.

Art, like music and dance, is found everywhere in Mexico. To most Mexicans, churches are works of art. Over hundreds of years, Mexican artists have decorated their churches with gold, paintings, and statues. The Aztecs used gold to embroider clothing and sandals, while they used cacao beans for money.

Mexican dancers perform a traditional folk dance.

Today, Mexicans still believe that gold should be where everyone can see it and enjoy it.

Throughout Mexico giant paintings called murals cover the walls of public buildings. They show the story of the Mexican people—the Aztecs, the Spanish conquest, the revolution—in pictures. Long ago the Aztecs painted pictures on their buildings, too. The pictures were their way of teaching all those who could not read.

A twentieth-century Mexican artist named Diego Rivera studied the Aztecs' art. He learned how to make their bright colors—green, red, yellow, and

More than 7 million stones were used to create this mural. It covers the central library building of the National Autonomous University of Mexico in Mexico City.

turquoise—from insect oils, sap, and natural earth colors. Mexicans call him the "soul" of their country's mural art.

Many treasures from Mexico's past are kept in museums. The biggest is the National Museum of Anthropology in Mexico City. All kinds of statues, bowls, jewelry, and other objects are displayed there to show how the Indians used to live. There is even a large model of Tenochtitlán, the fabled Aztec city. Seeing its gardens, palaces, temples, and busy canals, Cortés called it the "most beautiful city in the world."

An old Mexican saying explains that "to understand Mexico, you must understand the Indians." Mexicans are very interested in their Indian past, and they have done much to preserve it. Still, they don't spend all their time thinking about the past, for they are too busy living today.

One thing millions of Mexicans do today is to go to the movies. Mexico has a large film industry that turns out more than one hundred new movies each year. One of the best known actors is Cantinflas, whose real name is Mario Moreno. Mexicans flock to see him as the *pelado*, the very clever street beggar from the poorest part of Mexico City.

Telenovelas, or what we call soap operas, are very popular on Mexican television. They are shown once a week for a year or so, and then a new story comes on. "Simplemente María" was an all time favorite.

Small children enjoy comics and cartoons. Condorito is a man with a bird head who gets into all sorts of funny situations with his family and friends. But the biggest hero is the mindreader, Kaliman. When parts of stories come out each Monday, boys race to find out who their hero is helping. Girls rush to buy *fotonovelas.* They smile and cry as they read the love stories told in pictures.

The paseo, the tapatío, the siesta, and large, close families are all part of the manners and ways of Mexicans. The way people look and dress and where they live may vary in Mexico, but the way Mexicans think, feel, and dream is much the same.

3. From Pyramids to Oil Wells

While people in Europe still lived in caves and worked with tools of stone, Indians roamed and hunted in Mexico. Most scientists agree that the first North Americans, in scattered tribes, wandered across an icy bridge of land and snow from Asia to Alaska about twelve thousand years ago.

Being hunters, these early Indians may have been following the mammoths and buffalo. While many stayed in the snowy lands of the north, others stalked the giant game into the vast prairies of the United States. Slowly, over many years, some hunters headed south into Mexico.

Hunting was good in the thick Mexican forests. With plenty of wolves, deer, and bears to hunt, some early tribes stopped for a while and built huts. Women and girls gathered fruit and plants to eat. Seeds, skins, and pulp were tossed into big piles outside the huts. When sprouts burst forth from the garbage heaps, the Indians began to understand how to grow crops. They started to save seeds and plant them in the ground.

Farming changed the lives of the Indians. They stayed longer in one place and grew much of their food, but still made short trips into the forest to hunt. Now they had to learn how to get along with one another, choose leaders, and make laws. Wise men who told them about nature and the fierce gods of the wind, rain, and sun became their priests.

One group of these early Mexicans was the Olmecs. They built cities in the jungles along the gulf coast at about the same time the great pyramids of Egypt were built. In their cities they created beautiful stone carvings of people in flowing robes who were doing everyday things like chatting or playing sports.

The Olmecs grew corn and crushed the cacao bean to make a drink sweetened with honey. They molded clay pots into shapes of what they imagined their gods must look like. Cotton was gathered, spun, woven into cloth, and then sewn into clothing. The Olmecs are often called the "mother culture" of Mexico because all the other Indians learned from them.

One Indian nation that learned from the Olmecs was the Mayas in Yucatán. Like the Olmecs, the Mayas were farmers, and most of their diet was made up of corn. After soaking it, they pounded the corn between two stones. When it was crushed into a coarse meal, they added water to it and patted it into flat, round cakes. Since they only needed to spend seventy-six days a year growing the corn, the Mayas had lots of time left over to do other things.

Many of their activities had to do with the harvest. They invented a calendar that was more accurate than the Julian calendar used in Europe at that time. It showed three cycles: the sacred, the natural, and the planetary. The Mayas built domed observatories, or buildings equipped for viewing the heavens, entirely of stone. Peering through permanent, tiny openings, Mayan scientists followed the course of the sun, moon, and Venus. They knew that Venus had a year of 584 days and could predict eclipses of the moon.

The Mayas grouped buildings in such a way that by studying the line of the sunrise, they could predict the longest and shortest days of the year. Knowing these exact dates helped them keep track of the rainy season and the best time to plant their crops.

The men also spent time each year building such great cities as Uxmal, Palenque, and Chichén Itzá. Since Mayan cities were meant to honor the gods, only rulers and priests lived in them. The rest of the Mayas lived in small groups outside the cities.

We do not know why the Mayas left their cities. Scientists can find no trace of an earthquake, a volcanic eruption, or other natural disaster. There are no signs of war or death from disease. But suddenly, around A.D. 900, life stopped in the cities. Only scattered tribes stayed on, and no more great temples were built.

This Mayan pyramid was part of the sacred city of Chichén Itzá.

About the time the Mayas left their cities in Yucatán, the Toltec Indians established an empire high in the great Plateau of Mexico. They were a warlike people who conquered many of their neighboring tribes. After a while the Toltecs conquered the remaining Mayan people seven hundred miles away and took over the old city of Chichén Itzá. From the

Mayas they learned much about mathematics and astronomy.

People related to the Toltecs, the Teotihuacanos, built giant pyramids honoring the sun and moon in Teotihuacán ("House of the Gods") to the northeast of modern day Mexico City. Towering more than 200 feet (61 meters) above a dry plain, the Pyramid of the Sun still stands today. The Toltecs also built huge pyramids and elaborate temples in Tula, their beautiful capital.

When small bands from a tribe in the north wandered into Tula, they were very impressed by the city and its people. They tried to learn all they could from the powerful Toltecs.

Before long great numbers of these people, who called themselves *Azteca* or *Mexica*, traveled south in search of a new home. The wandering Indians caused so much trouble that neighboring tribes kept driving them out of their territories. They finally settled in the marshy swamps of Lake Texcoco where no one else wanted to live. At this time the large, shallow lake was full of snakes.

The Aztecs were delighted to live there because snake meat was one of their favorite foods. Eagerly, they caught the snakes and roasted them over campfires. Soon they built a nine-mile-long dam to separate the salt water of the lake from the fresh water flowing in from streams. From their *chinampas*, or

Built by the Teotihuacanos, the giant Pyramid of the Sun towers over Teotihuacán, the "City of the Gods."

floating gardens, in the fresh waters, they harvested all their vegetables. And in the marshes they found algae, water-fly eggs, grasshoppers, ducks, and geese.

About 1325 the Aztecs began to build Tenochtitlán, their great capital, on an island in Lake Texcoco. In the center of the city rose the palaces of rulers and the temples of priests. Beyond them lived the warriors and merchants. In the outer, marshy ring, in floating huts, lived the farmers.

There was great wealth in Tenochtitlán. As the

Aztecs fought many wars and conquered tribes in much of Mexico, they took thousands of slaves and demanded goods from the rest. The great Aztec marketplace brimmed with pottery, woven baskets and mats, the finest cloth, rope, feathers, gold, silver, precious stones, and fish and fowl from every region. Warriors captured in battle were offered as human sacrifices to the Aztec gods.

This was the great empire that Hernán Cortés, the Spanish explorer, found in 1519. Captain Grijalva had first learned of a rich land to the west when he sailed along the eastern coast of Mexico. His reports reached the Spanish colonial governor in Cuba, who asked his friend, Cortés, to lead an expedition in search of this land.

Cortés had dreamed of such an adventure ever since he was a boy. He was only eight years old when Columbus first sailed to America. Stories of treasure and strange, new lands filled his head as he grew up. His father wanted him to study law, but Cortés left school and joined the army in search of glory.

Naturally, Cortés was thrilled by the chance to explore the rich Aztec empire. He set out with eleven ships, six cannons, fifteen horses, and about six hundred men. At the first place he landed in Yucatán, he found deserted villages and shrines. And out from the brush came a Spaniard named Aguilar who had been shipwrecked years earlier and now spoke Maya.

At Cortés's next stop, after a brief battle with a Mayan tribe, he took several slaves from the chief. Luckily for Cortés, one of them was a young woman named Malinche. She had been captured from an Aztec tribe as a small girl and spoke Náhuatl, the Aztec language. Now Cortés was ready. He could speak Spanish to Aguilar who spoke Mayan to Malinche who spoke Náhuatl. Cortés could talk to the Aztecs!

Sailing farther up the coast, the Spaniards landed at what is now Veracruz. Frightened Tabascan Indians carrying spears and arrows spied at them from behind trees. The Indians were terrified because they had never seen horses or guns before. When their arrows bounced off the Spaniards' steel armor and shields, they thought the strange white men were gods.

Since the Tabascans disliked the powerful Aztecs, they soon joined forces with Cortés on his march to Tenochtitlán. As the Spaniards journeyed inland, other tribes offered to join with them, too.

At Tenochtitlán, Cortés led his forces peacefully across the main causeway. Thousands of Aztecs paddled out in their canoes to watch them. Moctezuma II, the Aztec emperor, came out to greet Cortés. Tall and slender, Moctezuma walked in the shade of a canopy embroidered in gold and silver, fringed with pearls, and held aloft by servants. Glittering robes draped his body, and his feet were clad in sandals of pure gold. Four-foot-long, green-gold plumes of the quetzal bird swept back from his headdress.

Cortés seized Moctezuma and held him as a prisoner. Later, after an Aztec revolt, the Spanish soldiers destroyed Tenochtitlán and killed thousands of Aztecs.

In two years Cortés conquered Mexico. Within twenty-five years, Spanish explorers claimed land from California to Texas, all along the gulf coast to Florida, and south to Panama. The whole colony was called New Spain, and a viceroy was sent from Spain to rule it.

As explorers and soldiers returned from expeditions, they were given land grants called *encomiendas*. The Indians remained on the land, but they worked for the new owners. Priests moved in among the Indians and taught them Spanish, how to read and write, and the ways of Christianity. Over the years, millions of Indians were baptized as Roman Catholics. In private, though, many of them continued to worship their old gods.

The people of New Spain were divided into four main groups. The Spaniards, called *peninsulares*, came from Spain to rule. The *criollos*, or creoles, the

Spanish explorers and missionaries established settlements in what is now the American Southwest. This settlement, the San Juan Mission, was founded near present-day San Antonio.

children of Spaniards born in New Spain, owned great ranches and farms, but they could not hold a high government post. The *mestizos*, of Spanish and Indian ancestry, worked as farmers, craftspeople, and laborers. The Indians were forced to work in the fields and in the gold and silver mines.

For nearly three hundred years, life in New Spain was quiet and unchanged. Sixty-three viceroys ruled the vast colony. One opened a college for Indian youths, and another set up the first printing press in the New World. The National University was established in 1553. Viceroys also settled fights between the Indians and the creoles who owned the encomiendas.

Even though many creoles were wealthy landowners, they opposed Spanish rule. By law, they were not allowed to grow grapes, olives, or tobacco. Trade with any other country was forbidden, and only Spanish ships could sail into port with goods for trade. Most of all, they grew tired of the Spaniards' control over their government.

The first declaration of independence was made on September 16, 1810. It took place in the little town of Dolores where there lived a poor parish priest named Miguel Hidalgo. The son of an old creole family, Father Hidalgo was once the head of a university. But he wanted so much to help the poor that he went to Dolores and lived among the Indians.

Hidalgo tried to teach the Indians how to grow crops and make things for themselves. Against the law, he sent for grapes and olive trees. He planted mulberry trees for silkworms, but Spanish soldiers came and tore them out.

Father Hidalgo became angry and joined a discussion group with some of the creoles in Dolores. They planned a revolt, but someone told the Spaniards about their plans. Father Hidalgo acted quickly. He ran to the church, tolled the bells, and cried out his famous *grito* for independence. Soon many Indians and mestizos, carrying sticks and machetes, gathered at the church to join him. As they marched to free Mexico from Spain, an army of farmers, Indians, and other village priests joined them.

The rebellion grew. Father Hidalgo and his men beat back the Spanish troops in a fierce battle in Guanajuato. His army of untrained followers fought its way to Mexico City. There Father Hidalgo hesitated, and his forces were defeated by the Spanish soldiers. He was captured and killed by the Spaniards. Today, Mexicans call him the father of their country.

The struggle for independence did not end with the death of Father Hidalgo. José Morelos, one of Hidalgo's men, organized a trained army and won many victories over the Spaniards. Like Hidalgo,

A mural shows Father Miguel Hidalgo.

Morelos was captured and shot. The state of Morelos was named after him, as well as the city of Morelia.

The war went on until 1821 when Mexico finally became independent. Then a new period of confusion began as Mexicans split into two groups, each with its own ideas about what kind of government the country should have. One group, the liberals, was made up of the poor, the men of Hidalgo's army, and those who wanted to help them. The other group, the conservatives, was made up mostly of wealthy Mexicans, including many creoles. For many years these two groups fought each other for power.

A military leader, Agustín de Iturbide, took control and declared himself emperor. Just ten months later, he was forced out by an army general, Antonio López de Santa Anna.

Santa Anna was in and out of power eleven times during the next thirty-three years. He fought the Texans at the Alamo. Later, when he was defeated by Sam Houston, he signed a treaty that made Texas an independent country. Ten years later, Mexico fought a war with the United States in which it lost California and much of what is now the American Southwest. Finally, in 1855, Santa Anna was driven from power by the liberals, and Benito Juárez, their leader, headed a new government.

Often called the "Abraham Lincoln" of his country, Benito Juárez was the first Mexican Indian to become president. He grew up in Oaxaca, the ancient home of the Zapotec Indians. A poor boy, he ran errands and did odd jobs in the marketplace to earn money. Since he was bright and energetic, a priest offered to teach him. He became a lawyer, and then governor of Oaxaca. People respected him because he was honest and believed in laws.

As president, Juárez made some laws that angered wealthy Mexicans so much that they led a revolt. He wanted to give land back to the Indians and break up the large estates owned by the creoles and the Roman Catholic church. After a civil war between the liberals and the conservatives, the country had no money left to pay its debts to foreign countries.

The French army invaded and conquered Mexico. Napoleon III, the French ruler, named Maximilian of the Austrian royal family to serve as the emperor. For three years Maximilian and his wife, Carlotta, ruled the Empire of Mexico. French soldiers sent by Napoleon guarded their splendid palace on a hill in what is now Chapultepec Park in Mexico City. Finally, in 1867, the United States pressured the French to pull out and sail back to France. When they did, the Mexicans rose up against Maximilian and shot him.

Benito Juárez came back to power. He started many schools for the Indians and tried again to break up some of the huge *haciendas*, or farms, of the creoles. Four years after his return, he died. Juárez was so greatly loved and mourned by his people that his Reform Laws were made part of the Mexican constitution.

Several years later, Porfirio Díaz, a mestizo general, seized power. Díaz started a crash program to change Mexico into a modern country. Factories, new railroads, and huge public building projects sprang up everywhere. Harbors were dredged, and broad boulevards like the ones in Paris were built. Mansions lined the tree-shaded streets. The lovely Palace of Fine Arts was built with three kinds of marble, glass domes, and statues of Mexican heroes.

A new Mexico showed its face to the world. Yet in the countryside, Indian lands were being sold, and the people were angry. Díaz organized a police force to quiet them. He hired toughs and bandits known as *rurales*. Dressed in tight leather pants, short jackets, and wide hats, they waved pistols and rode fine, fast horses. The rurales kept a close watch on the poor.

Díaz and his friends ruled Mexico for thirty-five years. Since he didn't allow any real campaigning against him in "elections," he always won. Unrest grew. Finally, new elections were called.

The year was 1910, exactly one hundred years after the revolt led by Hidalgo. A man named Francisco Madero wrote a book about political freedom and decided to run against Díaz. Even though Madero was from one of the wealthiest families in Mexico, his greatest goal was to help the poor. People read his book and listened to him as he traveled all over the country. Because he became widely popular, Díaz had him arrested and thrown in jail. When he was released, he fled to the United States and continued to speak out aginst Díaz.

Uprisings swelled all over Mexico. In the north, Pancho Villa, who had once been an outlaw, led an army of bandits and the poor. They robbed the rich, rustled cattle, and fought the *federales*, the government soldiers. Villa's hit-and-run tactics made him a famous military leader during the revolution.

Mexicans loved Pancho Villa. A heavy-set man with a deep, roaring laugh, he rode a large black horse called Lucifer. With cartridges criss-crossed over his chest, twirling his pistol in the air, he always tricked the federales and disappeared into the wilderness.

Emiliano Zapata led more rebels in the south. Because he believed that the land should belong to the people who worked it, Indian workers rallied around him. Together, in small bands, they sacked great sugar plantations in the state of Morelos. Zapata tried to take the land away from the wealthy land-owners and give it back to the Indians who farmed it. His ideas later became part of the Mexican constitution.

The revolution lasted until 1917, when a new constitution was written. It gave the government control over farmlands, oil wells, education, and the Roman Catholic church. All land was declared the property of the government, and plans were made to give it back to small farmers for as long as they could work it. No one would own the land. Instead, it would belong to the village, and everyone would share in using it. This was the way of the ancient Indians. Other laws were made to establish labor unions and to give workers more pay and shorter hours. Presidents could stay in office for only one term.

The basic aims and ideas of the revolution were written in the new constitution. Finally, the bloody struggle between the wealthy and the poor ended. A new period began in which many Mexicans worked together to make the dreams of the revolution come true.

Before long a new group emerged to carry out the revolutionary program. Instead of two fighting groups—one of the wealthy, one of the poor—the new one combined the two somewhere in the middle. Later this new group formed a political party to carry out its programs. Now known as the Institutional Revolutionary Party, it has won every national election since the 1920s.

Some of the biggest changes began when Plutarco Elías Calles became president in 1924. For ten years he gave land back to the poor who once worked the great plantations. The new farms, called *ejidos*, were owned and worked by everyone, and the profits were shared by all.

Lázaro Cárdenas gave back even more land than Calles to the poor. Then, in 1938, Cárdenas made the United States and Great Britain very angry when he ordered a takeover of all seventeen of their oil companies in Mexico. He offered to pay the companies for their losses, but they were not satisfied. Relations between the United States and Mexico were very poor during those years. After World War II, however, the two nations became friendly once more.

Mexican industry has grown rapidly since World War II. The biggest manufacturing business is textiles. Huge factories busily turn out bolts of cloth, much of it for export. Next in output come beer, tequila, glass, cement, paper, and automobiles. The oldest industries, steel and iron, still thrive.

Yet agriculture is still the most important industry in Mexico. Cotton and corn are the major crops, and sugar cane and coffee are important, too.

Tequila, an important Mexican export, is produced in large batches in modern plants.

While industry has grown, until 1978 the biggest source of income for Mexico was tourism. Then huge new oil strikes made oil the country's number one export. Using the new oil wealth, the government began to carry out expensive programs to make life better for all Mexicans. But the recent worldwide drop in oil prices dealt a blow to Mexico. By 1982 an economic crisis had begun, the worst in seventy years.

In that year the value of Mexico's currency, the peso, had to be lowered because of the nation's economic troubles. Another big problem was the prices of everyday items, which kept going higher and higher. At one point the price of tortillas doubled in three weeks. The situation was so bad that Mexico had to arrange emergency loans to pay its foreign debts. Those debts are now among the highest of any country in the world.

Today some of the big development projects started during the oil boom are at a standstill. As a result, many workers have lost their jobs. Some experts say that Mexico must create 800,000 new jobs each year to meet the needs of the young people who enter its work force. Since the nation has one of the highest birth rates in the world, that need for jobs will grow even more in the years to come.

On July 4, 1982, Mexicans elected a new president, Miguel de la Madrid. He promised to cut government spending, hold down rising prices, and try to repay the foreign debt. The challenge for the new president is to deal with all the problems facing Mexico today, and to keep the giant of the south on the road to growth.

4. Stories From a Proud Past

As Mexicans uncover ancient ruins and other traces from their past, they learn more about the great myths and legends of old. Each new find is a national treasure. It is like a piece of a great puzzle that helps to complete the picture of a time long gone.

Mexican boys and girls hear all the famous tales of ancient times, both from their relatives and in school. Even the names of many places remind them of their Indian ancestors. Children marvel at the graceful temples and read stories about the many powerful gods of the Mayas and Aztecs. When they see the tall, rugged pyramids, they imagine what it was like to live in the days of the mighty Toltecs. They wonder what their Indian ancestors felt and believed.

We all have a need to explain ourselves and the world around us. Just like us, the ancient Indians in Mexico wondered about themselves and asked the same hard questions we ask today. Where do we come from? How did we get here? They also asked some of the same questions about nature. Why does it rain? What makes a volcano erupt? Why do we have floods and sometimes drought?

Since life on earth was often harsh, the ancient

This drawing shows a Mayan storm god as it appears on a temple carving (illustration by Denzil Smith).

Indians looked to the stars for answers. They found that the sun and moon follow an exact path. These patterns gave them a sense of order and well-being.

To the Mayas, the sky was filled with hundreds of gods. They lived in the clouds, high above the mountains. Some of the most powerful ones were the gods of day and night, and the gods of heaven, hell, wind, war, and death. Most important were the gods of the harvest and the rain. Their job was to see that the rains fell on time and that the crops grew.

Other gods moved time. Years, months, and even days of the week had a god. A month passed before the god carried the time on his back as a burden. At the end of each month, hundreds of Mayas in bright costumes prayed and danced so that the next god would take over the job of moving time.

A special river god was said to live in the water, deep in the giant pit at Chichén Itzá. To please the god, the Mayas threw precious stones and things that they most prized into the sacred well. Sometimes, when there was a drought, people were thrown into the well as a sacrifice to the god.

Since it was a great honor to be chosen, the person never fought back. At sunrise, fancy processions snaked their way to the well's edge. After calling to the god to tell him what was happening, the person was tossed into the air and splashed into the water sixty feet below.

If the person lived, he or she was pulled out of the well at noon. Then all the people gathered round to hear what the river god had said. Anyone who lived through the ordeal of the sacred well was treated almost like a god.

The Mayas believed that their gods were wise, but they did not know how they would act. If the gods were angry, they might bring floods or drought to destroy the crops. If the gods were kept happy, they

Like the ancient Mayas, these people climb the steep steps of a pyramid at Chichén Itzá.

would be kind to the people. To please them, the Mayas held great ceremonies on top of their pyramids.

People streamed up the steep, narrow steps to the upper platform. Eyes fixed downward, hands clutching bowls heaped with jewels and food, they approached with their offering. The priest took it and held it high in the air to show the gods, and then he placed it in the sacred fires. Hoping and fearing, crowds waited for the priest to tell them the message from the gods about the future.

When the gods were not busy making everything work, they liked to turn themselves into animals and run around on earth. Animals were very special to the Mayas because any animal might really be a god in disguise. To them, the jaguar was a symbol of power. The snake was wise about things of the earth. The turtle was magical because it could live both in the water and in the air. Each Maya felt close to a certain animal and believed that he or she shared a soul with it.

One of the greatest things the Mayan gods had done was to create human beings. Since they had some trouble doing it, they had to try four different times before they got it right. The first time the gods scooped up mud and molded some men, but the men dissolved in water. Next they carved men of wood who were so hollow and dry that they floated away in a flood. Then the gods made ugly, cruel creatures that didn't go away. The Mayas believed that monkeys were their descendants.

Finally, the gods picked some corn from a special place beneath a mountain. They ground it and mixed it with water to make a soft mush which they shaped and hardened. This mixture was the beginning of humankind.

Four men were created who lived in a paradise. They were all-knowing and all-seeing. Wherever the men stood, they could see the whole world at once. Because they were perfect, the gods became jealous and blew mist into their eyes. The men lost their great powers and could see only things close to them.

The time of paradise had ended. Since then, believed the Mayas, the whole world had been flooded several times, and humans had to struggle to stay alive. The kind of work they did in this life decided where they would go after they died.

Up in the great Plateau of Mexico, the Aztecs had their own view of the way human beings had been created. They believed that the whole universe had been made and destroyed four times. The Aztecs called each universe a sun.

The first sun ended in a great flood, and all the people turned into fish. The second burned up in a huge fire. This time humans changed into birds and flew away. The third sun ended with a fierce wind in which the people became monkeys and clung to the trees. The fourth sun saw a race of giants who were eaten by jaguars.

Two gods decided to try again and hurled themselves into a great fire. Two bright, fiery balls rose in the sky. One was the fifth sun, which was the time of the Aztecs. The other was the moon. Since it was just as bright as the sun, the rest of the gods took a rabbit and stuck it in the moon to dim the light. Even today,

Mexicans say, if you look carefully, you will see the outline of the rabbit in the moon.

According to Aztec beliefs, the gods had parents. The father ruled the heavens, and the mother ruled the earth. Each of their four sons was given a part of the world to control.

Camaxtli, the first son, ruled the east. He was always dressed in red because the east was red in Aztec picture writing.

The second son was the mean, black Tezcatlipoca, or Smoking Mirror. He controlled the north.

Quetzalcoatl, the god of wisdom and kindness, ruled the west. He was also the creator of humankind. When he gathered the bones of the dead giants of the fourth sun and sprinkled his own blood over them, humans sprang up. They were the first people of the fifth sun, the original Aztecs.

Huitzilopochtli, the god of the south, was the special god of the Aztecs. Aztec stories say he ordered the people to leave Aztlan, or the "place of the herons," their original home, to search for a new home. They carried a statue of him on their backs as they traveled. He gave them messages through their priest and told them to change their name to *Mexica.*

First the Aztecs wandered into the dry lands of the north, but Huitzilopochtli ordered them to keep traveling. Next they went south to Tula where they

Huitzilopochtli, the special god of the Aztecs (illustration by Denzil Smith).

met the Toltecs. Again, their god told them to move on. Once into the Valley of Mexico, he led them into the reeds and rushes. There, he said, they must find an eagle on a cactus eating a snake while warming itself in the sun. At the place where they found this sign, they must build their new home.

In the marshes of Lake Texcoco, the Aztecs found the sign they sought. The eagle and snake are now the national symbol of Mexico and appear on the Mexican flag.

Huitzilopochtli and the many gods played a part in every part of life in the Aztec world. A warrior would not go to battle if the signs were not good for him. A woman would not mold a clay pot unless the stars told her the time was right. There were gods watching over the crops and flowers. Silversmiths, potters, and weavers had their own god. Every community had one, too.

Huitzilopochtli, the god of sun and war, was all important to the Aztecs. Each day, they believed, he climbed into the sun and carried it across the sky with the help of dead warriors known as "'eagle men." At noon women who died while giving birth to a child joined in and helped carry the sun to sunset.

When Huitzilopochtli met the gods of darkness, he fought with them. They always won, and he was forced to spend hours in the worlds under the earth. These were the dark, fearful hours. In the morning, only if he was strong, he beat them and rose once more to move the sun on its path in the sky.

Of all the Indian gods and the stories about them, perhaps the most famous is the legend of Quetzal-coatl, the god of wind, wisdom, and goodness. His name means "feathered serpent" and comes from the words *quetzal* ("bird of paradise") and *coatl* ("serpent"). Paintings of Quetzalcoatl show him wearing a fancy headdress of blue-green quetzal feathers and the mask of a serpent face.

According to the Aztecs and the Mayas, Quetzalcoatl once lived among the Toltecs as a man. He would have walked the earth in Mexico about the same time the legendary King Arthur hunted in the forests of Gaul. Quetzalcoatl was tall, with fair skin and a beard. He directed the cutting of the giant stones of the great pyramids of Tula and taught the people how to carve and decorate the huge rocks. Stories of the beauty of Tula spread throughout the land. Quetzalcoatl was so loved and admired that the year of his birthday, known as "1-reed," became a time of celebration.

This wise and good god taught the people many things—how to grind corn, weave mats and cloth, and make bowls from clay. He also gave them their calendar. Above all, Quetzalcoatl taught that human sacrifices to the gods were bad. He wanted the people to learn about nature, not be afraid of it. His teachings angered Smoking Mirror, his brother, who wanted men to fear the gods.

Smoking Mirror drove Quetzalcoatl away from the Toltecs, and many of his loyal warriors went with him. They stayed with the Mixtec Indians in Cholula. There they built the tallest pyramid in all of Mexico. It was so tall that they called it the "man-made mountain." But Smoking Mirror would not let Quetzalcoatl rest. He chased him out of Cholula.

Quetzalcoatl would not fight Smoking Mirror. Instead, he carved a great canoe and sailed out into the ocean. He told the Indians that he would return one day in the year 1-Reed.

After Quetzalcoatl left, the stalks of corn grew thin and lean, and the soil dried and cracked. Once again the Indians were afraid and hungry. They awaited his return. Wise men and priests studied the stars and calendars to determine when the year 1-Reed would fall. All agreed that it could be only one of two years, 1467 or 1519 in our calendar.

When 1467 passed, the Aztecs believed that Quetzalcoatl would return for sure in 1519. They were expecting him the year Cortés arrived, a tall, fair-skinned man with a beard. Surely, the Aztecs thought, this strange-looking man must be Quetzalcoatl, and they greeted him as a god.

After the arrival of the Spaniards and their priests, the Aztecs accepted the Christian teachings about the one God. Yet in many ways, Aztec beliefs mixed with Christianity and created a special kind of Mexican religion. Just as the Aztecs had looked for the sign of the eagle eating the snake, they now awaited a new message.

Roman Catholics believe that it came only twelve years after Cortés landed. As an Indian named Juan Diego was climbing over the Tepeyac Hill near Mexico City one day, he smelled sweet perfume and heard soft music.

When he looked up, he saw a beautiful, dark-haired maiden surrounded by a bright halo of light. A voice told Juan Diego that she wished to have a great cathedral built on that very spot. Juan Diego was so excited that he ran to see the bishop and tell him what he had seen. The bishop told him that he must have proof.

Feeling sad, Juan Diego returned to the hill. Suddenly, he saw the beautiful maiden again. A voice told him to pick some roses from the hill to bring to the bishop. Juan Diego looked about at the dry and barren hill—only cactus grew. But as he climbed higher and searched among the rocks, to his joy he found a thorny bush full of blooming roses. He picked them and wrapped them in his *tilma,* or cloak.

When Juan Diego appeared the second time before the bishop, he unfolded the tilma, and the roses tumbled to the floor. On his cloak was a glowing picture of the Virgin Mary.

A cathedral was built in honor of the Virgin of

Guadalupe on that very hill. It still stands today. Each year thousands of the poor and ill, some on crutches and others crawling, go there to seek cures from Mexico's patron saint.

All over Mexico there are tiny shrines—on a hillside, alongside a road, or in a clump of trees. A statue stands with freshly cut flowers, and perhaps a candle, fruit, or cakes. That spot is special to the Indian people because they believe someone has seen an image or heard a voice of a saint. The Indians feel very close to the saints and often hear messages from spirits.

While much of Mexican life centers around religion, some legends have been created about people who were involved in more worldly matters. Malinche, the young Indian woman who helped Cortés against the Aztecs, appears in many tales as a traitor and witch. When the rain pounds on thatched roofs, and the wind howls through the trees, many Mexicans will say that it is the sad weeping of Malinche. To them, *malinchismo*, being unfaithful to the mother country, is one of the worst crimes a Mexican can commit.

Mexicans also remember a Chinese princess who was kidnapped by pirates and sold in the slave market. In Puebla she wore the simple dress of the Indian women and dedicated her life to helping the poor. Her style of clothing later became the national dress of Mexico. A white cotton blouse with lots of embroidery, a brightly colored sash, and a full, bright red and green skirt is called the *china poblana*—"the Chinese woman from Puebla."

Above all, Mexicans enjoy exciting stories about the dashing, romantic bandit. One of the most popular is about the daring Lorenzo. In the mountains one day, while out to rob travelers on the old highway to Puebla, he spied a beautiful señorita on her way back to her father's hacienda. Lorenzo fell instantly in love. For weeks he could not sleep or eat; he only dreamed of the señorita.

Finally, his love overcame him. With his men he charged into the hacienda one night and swept the girl onto his horse. They rode off into the night. Lorenzo planned a wedding, but just before it took place, the girl's father attacked the camp. He shot Lorenzo and carried the girl back home. Now, each year, Lorenzo is remembered in a great fiesta in Puebla.

During the Revolution of 1910, the adventures of the bandit heroes were very popular. Pancho Villa, whose real name was Doroteo Arango, was one of the best known. In those days there was no television or radio or even newspapers in country towns. Messengers traveled from town to town on horseback and sang exciting songs about the battles. Some of these songs, the *corridos*, such as "La Cucaracha" and "Adelita," are still favorites today.

When the songsters told of the death of Pancho Villa, Mexicans did not believe them. Even today, the poor people and farmers claim that Pancho Villa still lives. They say you can see him riding in the mountains on moonlit nights. Astride his big black horse, Lucifer, he ducks the federales as his roaring laugh echoes through the hills.

Emiliano Zapata, the revolutionary hero of the south, is still talked about in the sugar fields of Morelos. Men chopping cane with machetes will tell you that Zapata never died. Some say they have seen him on his great white horse. They claim he is hiding and waiting to return to help the Indians in their struggle for freedom. Meanwhile, he rides under the stars, crying out "land and liberty."

The stories of ancient peoples and romantic heroes are passed along over the years. But times change. Today Mexicans no longer fear the anger of vengeful gods as did the ancient Mayas and Aztecs. Now many look to science to answer their questions. They study nature and find patterns and order in the world. Yet in a way, the great heroes of the past still live. Their deeds are remembered, and their spirits live on in the way the people think of their country today.

5. Families, Fun, and Fiestas

In Mexico's cities and towns, one fiesta follows another throughout the year. Food stalls pop up on the walkways of the central plazas. The smell of crackling *chicharrones*, beans, and tortillas make everyone hungry. Giant pots of soup bubble and steam, while fresh cut watermelons, papayas, bananas, and strawberries are heaped high. Children chew on chunks of sliced sugar cane. Vendors hold puffy, gaily colored balloons up high, streamers flying, and call out to passersby. Church bells toll, firecrackers pop, and young people laugh loudly as they play.

Soft melodies of marimbas, flutes, and guitars or the brassy blasts of trumpets ripple through the air. The town band tunes up in the *kiosque*, while under the jacaranda trees, snugly wrapped in their mothers' *rebozos*, small children nap. Little girls lead toddlers by the hand, and boys play hide and seek. Buses filled with people from nearby villages rumble into the square through the happy crowds.

As night falls, sparkling fireworks burst in a shower of bright light. Fiery pinwheels twirl as pops and explosions fill the cool night air. Everyone joins in the excitement of a fun-filled Mexican fiesta.

(Above) *For these children, a fiesta is a time for good food, fun, and games.* (Left) *A happy young girl munches a sweet slice of sugar cane.*

Just beyond the plaza, behind the thick walls of homes, many more private celebrations take place among families. Each important event in the lives of family members is marked by a gathering of the whole family. Many of the celebrations are religious and have to do with the different stages of growing and learning that all Mexicans must go through.

The first celebration in a child's life is his or her baptism. Aunts and uncles, brothers and sisters, and all the family gathers at the church. The tiny baby is carried in for the priest's blessing with holy water. The baptism is usually the first outing for a Mexican baby because most mothers will not take their baby out before it has been baptized.

A very special time in the lives of Mexican children is their first communion. By the time they reach the age of seven, children are asked to think about the good and bad things they do. Have they been mean to their brother or sister? Did they disobey their mother or father? Have they tried their best to help someone in need? Then, when they recognize the bad things they have done, they tell their sins to a priest and promise to try not to do them again.

After this first confession, children receive the bread and wine of their first communion. Christians believe that this ceremony gives meaning to Christ's death on the cross. Parents look on proudly as their children parade slowly into the church, heads bowed, and hands pressed together pointing upward. Many children carry lighted candles, catechism books, and rosary beads with them as signs of their faith. For them their first communion is a big step in life.

After the church service, the family gathers together for food and fun. Parents are so proud of their children that they hug them. Plates filled with special foods are put on the table, and everyone joins in the celebration.

About five years later, when young people are twelve years old, they take their next big step in life, confirmation. They study hard and learn about Jesus and Roman Catholic beliefs. Then they take a test to show what they have learned. At last they are welcomed into the church as young adults. To celebrate, the family gathers for parties with lots of food and music.

The next stage in life is usually marriage. Weddings are often big, fancy affairs. Little girls like to dress up in long, pastel-colored gowns and wear flowers in their hair. Bouquets in hand, they march slowly down the aisle, leading the bride's procession. Altar boys help the priest during the wedding ceremony. Afterwards, rows of tables fill with well-wishers for the reception.

Just as family celebrations mark the stages of life,

national fiestas fill the calendar each year. Many of these, also, are religious. Before Lent, the forty weekdays leading up to Easter, begins, Mexicans enjoy the happy carnival season.

The city of Puebla is known for its carnival fiesta honoring the bandit Lorenzo. Actors play out his legendary kidnapping of the lovely señorita. A young boy dresses up as the señorita and leaps from a balcony onto the bandit's horse. Onlookers enjoy the battle between Lorenzo and the girl's father. Finally, the bandit is shot, and the play ends as flames destroy a little shack like the one at Lorenzo's camp in the mountains.

After the noisy, merry carnival celebrations, everything quiets down. Mexicans take the Lenten season seriously. During these six weeks they give up something that is really important to them. Children promise not to eat candy, ice cream, or whatever their favorite treat may be. Roman Catholics believe giving up their favorite things helps show that their faith is real and honest. They also believe that this sacrifice makes them stronger and better able to control themselves.

Lent ends with the religious celebrations of Holy Week. Candlelight processions and fiestas fill each day. On Good Friday, in small towns, people act out the Passion plays about the suffering and death of Jesus. On Saturday, in the streets of bigger towns and cities, young people explode large, papier-mâché heads of Judas, filled with gunpowder. These heads are used in much the same way that Americans use fireworks on the Fourth of July.

On Easter Sunday, families dress up in their finest and go to church. Girls wear straw hats with flowers, or perhaps a lace veil, gloves, and shiny shoes. Some wear tiny pearl earrings, while others may pin corsages on their dresses. Boys wear their best clothes and stand straight and tall.

After church Mexicans spend the day relaxing, eating, and enjoying themselves. Some families prefer to picnic outdoors, while others go to a bullfight. By early evening the central plazas are filled with people who have come to play and listen to band concerts.

At different times of the year, in all parts of the country, there are festivals honoring the Virgin of Guadalupe. But the biggest fiesta of all is the one at the cathedral built on Tepeyac Hill where Juan Diego had his vision. Thousands of people travel there each year during the first week of December. A huge fair with food, rides, balloons, and fun for everyone takes place all around the church.

There are no witches or pumpkins in Mexico for Halloween. Instead, Mexicans celebrate the Day of the Dead in honor of those who have died. Bakers place signs in their windows announcing *pan de*

A vendor displays his balloons for the people who have come to a Mexico City plaza to listen to a band concert.

muerto, or "bread of the dead." It's a raisin-filled bread with pastry crossbones baked across the top, or sugar icing dribbled on in the shape of bones. Candy stores and market stalls feature *dulces,* or sweets, in the form of skulls.

Mexican Indians in villages decorate little altars in their shacks. Since they believe that dead relatives visit on this day, they cook the favorite meals of the dead and leave them for the unseen visitors to eat. Fruit and sweet cakes are left for the dead children, who are called *angelitos,* or "little angels."

Throughout Mexico many families meet at cemeteries. Toys and candy are placed on the graves of children. Families talk about happy times and old memories, and no one is sad. At night tombstones glow with the light of candles, and the smell of incense hangs in the air.

In early November Mexicans begin to prepare for the Christmas season. Today, in some of the bigger department stores in cities, there are pictures of Santa Claus and Christmas trees. Most Mexicans, however, don't know about these things.

Christmas to Mexicans is the story of Mary and Joseph searching for an inn in Bethlehem. On the nine nights before Christmas, the people act out the search for a place for Jesus to be born in processions called *las posadas.* Holding candles and small statues of the holy family, children join in the posadas. Sometimes they balance a *nacimiento*, or nativity scene, between two poles and carry it like a stretcher.

From the main plaza, the line of pilgrims winds its way through the streets. The marchers sing carols that tell of Mary and Joseph's search. As they march, the pilgrims knock at eight closed doors. Finally, the ninth door swings open wide, and everyone enters. All join in songs and prayers, and then the whole group jams into the patio for food, fun, and dancing.

For children the best part of the posada is the breaking of the *piñata*. Overhead, hanging from a rope, is a big, clay jar filled with candies, fruits, nuts, and toys. Covered with brightly colored tissue paper, the piñata may look like a bull, an angel, a sheep, or another animal. All the children gather below it, and one of them is blindfolded. With a long stick in hand, the child swings out at the piñata, trying to break it open. When at last the piñata cracks open, everyone scrambles in and grabs what they can.

On Christmas Eve friends and family gather for a special dinner of turkey and a salad that is made of many kinds of fresh fruits. Then everyone goes to midnight mass for the Roman Catholic celebration of Christ's birth.

The traditional day for gift giving in Mexico is January 6. This is the twelfth day of Christmas when the three Magi arrived in Bethlehem with gifts for the Christ child. On the night before, children put their shoes outside their door or on a balcony before they go to bed. If they have been good, they will find the shoes filled with toys. But if they have been bad, they will find charcoal in them.

Families invite friends and relatives to celebrate the twelfth night by sharing a delicious bread called *Rosca de los Reyes.* Baked in a ring, this bread is filled with raisins, candied fruit, and nuts. The baker hides a tiny doll inside the batter before baking it. Then the guest who gets the piece with the doll inside must give another party on Feburary 2.

While some Christmas customs in Mexico are different from ours, other holidays are celebrated in much the same way. On New Year's Eve, for example, people have lively parties in their homes. They think about the past year and make many promises for the coming year. And just like us, they forget their promises very quickly.

Still other Mexican holidays are completely different from any of our own. Many of these have roots in old Indian customs, such as the special day in January for blessing animals. Children scrub their pets and decorate them with ribbons and bows. Then they go to the church where the priest sprinkles the animals with holy water to bless them for the year. In this way the old Aztec love and respect for animals lives on.

On the feast day of Corpus Christi, thousands of Mexican young people join in a procession to the huge Cathedral of Mexico at the Zócalo, or main plaza, in Mexico City. Girls dress in the red and green full skirts and white blouses of the china poblana.

On feast days many Mexicans gather at the Zócalo in Mexico City. The National Cathedral faces one side of the huge plaza.

Boys wear the white clothes of the campesino with *serapes*, or narrow blankets, over their shoulders. Many of the young people tote small wooden boxes on their backs supported by straps around their foreheads. They dress like the poor people and carry burdens as workers do in the marketplace and on farms. It is their way of remembering their Indian heritage.

Some Mexican celebrations have not changed since the days of the Aztecs. In parts of the mountains near Puebla and Veracruz, Indians still follow an ancient custom called *los voladores*, "the flying men." A tall pole, about sixty feet high, is set up, with a platform built on top. Five "fliers," dressed as birds, climb up the pole. One dances on the platform. The other four tie ropes around their legs and jump into the air, falling in wide circles around the pole. The rope is let out slowly as they sail downwards to the beating of drums and the soft, airy sounds of flutes.

Tradition says that the five fliers stand for the five suns of the Aztecs. The fifth sun stays on top, while the other four fly away and end. Perhaps the ceremony is the Indians' way of showing how "time flies."

Holidays from more recent times have been established to remember the great heroes of the Mexican past. José Morelos and Benito Juárez have national holidays in their honor. Like George Washington, Father Hidalgo has a holiday to celebrate his birthday. Mexicans recall both the writing of their constitution and the anniversary of the Revolution of 1910 with holidays.

Mexican Independence Day, September 16, is the biggest and noisiest of the holidays for national heroes. Military parades, a review of soldiers, and long speeches go on all day. In every city and town, the famous "grito" of Father Hidalgo, calling for independence, is read in the main plaza. Throughout the land, church bells toll, and fireworks explode.

In the National Palace, a huge, fancy buffet is spread out for honored guests. A team of cooks prepares a special dish for the dinner, called *chile en nogada.* Long, green chiles are stuffed with ground pork and spices, dipped in batter, and fried. A thick, white sauce is poured over the chiles and sprinkled with bright red pomegranate seeds. When a sprig of parsley is placed in the center, the dish has the three colors of the Mexican flag—red, white, and green.

All year long, fiestas play a big part in Mexican life. Whether Mexicans give a party at home or celebrate with many others in the local plaza, they share the same feeling of people enjoying other people. A fiesta is a time for laughing and smiling and eating and relaxing in the company of loved ones and friends.

6. *Good Food and Laughter Shared*

To most Mexicans, nothing is more important than the family. Close ties in large families have a long history that dates back to the Mayas, the Aztecs, and later, the Spaniards. Old customs are still passed on from parents to children, for many Mexicans treasure the old ways. Children grow up knowing that they are an important member of a strong and loyal group — their family. No matter what happens, they know that they will always be loved by their relatives.

The head of most Mexican families is the father. When important decisions are made, he has the last word. Children respect their fathers and are quick to show their love. In some homes even grown sons kiss their fathers on the cheek each morning as they greet.

Much of home life depends on the father's work schedule. Whether he commutes to an office in the city, minds a store in a small town, or plows fields in the mountains, the whole household lives according to his job. Mexican men don't like to change jobs or move their families away from the old neighborhood and friends.

Whatever her husband's work may be, a Mexican woman devotes most of her time to home, husband,

Shopping for a large family is a daily task for many Mexican women.

and children. Women believe that taking care of their families is the most important job in their lives. Even for the women who work at other jobs outside the home, their family comes first.

Since most Mexican families have six children or more, just running the house is no small task. Imagine what it would be like to keep house and plan meals for a family of ten! That's enough work to keep anyone busy cooking, cleaning, and shopping.

In the wealthiest families, the wife never does any housework. Instead, she directs a staff of maids, who are usually Indian women from the country. Each one has a special job. One cooks, washes clothes, and irons. Another sweeps floors, makes beds, and serves meals. The third scrubs and waxes and cleans bathrooms.

Even families that are not wealthy usually hire at least one maid to clean the house, change sheets, and do the laundry. Maids become part of the family and join in many of its activities. They watch TV soap operas and variety shows with the family. When they need a doctor's care, the *señora* pays the maid's bills.

In the poorest families, everyone has to help with the work. The older girls clean house and wash clothing, while younger sisters care for babies and do the dishes. Boys find some way to earn money, perhaps running errands or shining shoes. The children do all the chores while their parents are away at work.

As children grow up, they begin to think about getting married. Girls marry at a young age, sometimes at fifteen. By the time they are twenty, they have at least one, and probably two, children. Often their youngest brother or sister is the same age as their own child. When the whole family gets together, it's hard

Most Mexican women have one or two children by age twenty. Their youngest brothers and sisters may be about the same age as their own children.

to tell who is the mother and who is the sister.

Since supporting a family is a big responsibility, boys usually wait until they are in their twenties before thinking of marriage. Then they date girls much younger than themselves.

When it comes to dating, fathers are stern. They never allow their daughters to go out with a young man who has not introduced himself properly to the family first. Then he must ask permission to see the daughter and ask someone else to come with them on their date. A grandmother, an older sister, or perhaps even an uncle will escort a young woman and her admirer. Usually fathers prefer that daughters meet the sons of families that are already known to them.

Even after marrying, a Mexican woman keeps her father's name, and she adds her husband's name, too. In fact, most Mexicans use two last names— those of their father and of their mother or husband. If María Ortiz García marries Jorge López Marín, then their son, Manuel, will be named Manuel López Ortiz.

Unmarried women often live with their sisters and share in the household chores and cooking. Mothers-in-law live in, too. Grown-up couples complain about "mothers" bossing them around and talking all the time. But when they fix tasty meals and take care of the grandchildren, parents are glad that they live with them.

Whether wealthy or poor, the heart of every household is the kitchen. And when it comes to food, Mexican women take charge. Even if a maid does much of the cooking, the mother tells her what to prepare. Then she tastes it and seasons it herself.

Meals are the high points of the day. Early in the morning, the hungry family gathers at the table. Like Americans, Mexicans eat eggs for breakfast, but they like them to taste much more spicy.

If you want to wake up your mouth in the morning, try Mexican-style eggs sometime. Just beat some eggs with bits of finely chopped onion, tomato, and chile peppers, and then scramble them in butter or margarine. If you prefer fried eggs, try *huevos rancheros*. Place your sunny-side-up egg on top of a warmed tortilla, cover it with red chile sauce, and put some refried beans on the side. Refried beans aren't really fried at all, but cooked beans that are mashed and reheated.

When everyone is in a hurry for breakfast, Mexican mothers serve sweet rolls and papaya, pineapple, or strawberries. Parents drink big cups of *café con leche*, coffee mixed with milk. Children like hot chocolate sweetened with honey and a touch of cinnamon.

Mexicans eat their biggest meal of the day early in the afternoon, usually about two o'clock. Whenever possible, everyone comes home from work or school for the main meal. Since older, married children often stop by with their families, there can be as many as twenty people for dinner!

With two hours set aside for the midday meal, Mexicans take their time eating. They enjoy their food, and then relax or nap during the siesta.

Since preparing that much food can take hours, mothers go to the market early in the morning. In homes without refrigerators, women must shop every day. Rice, beans, and corn, once cooked, will keep for

Large, open-air markets are popular places to shop in Mexico's cities.

a few days, but meat, milk, and green vegetables must be fresh.

While American-style supermarkets are becoming more popular in cities, Mexican women still prefer the open-air markets. They like to buy their food directly from the farmers who grow it. Heaps of fresh squash, potatoes, peppers, and corn fill the marketplace tables. Shoppers pinch the green beans and squeeze the tomatoes. Then they talk over the price with the farmer.

Some of the vegetables are unknown north of the Mexican border. One, the pale-green *chayote*, is shaped like a pear. Another, the *jícama*, looks like a brown-skinned sugar beet on the outside, an apple on the inside, and tastes like a water chestnut.

The biggest markets in Mexico City and Guadalajara cover huge ten-block areas. More than two thousand stalls line the walkways. Vendors sell pots and pans, pottery and gadgets, and clothing that hangs displayed from wires. Shoppers choose from more than twenty different kinds of beans—black,

Many Mexicans shop in neighborhood stores like this one.

red, pink, purple, yellow, white, and speckled. Chiles come in many sizes and shapes, dried and fresh, hot and mild. Meat hangs on hooks out in the open and turns brown on the outside.

In the small country markets, everything is spread out on top of a cloth on cement floors. Tiny street and village markets often display their wares on a dirt road.

Back home from the market, vegetables must be scrubbed. The most careful mothers soak them in chemically treated water to kill germs and bacteria. Little girls help pick tiny stones from the dried beans. Since meat doesn't come sliced and wrapped in neat little packages the way we buy it, cooks slice it to size and trim off fat.

In Mexico there aren't many frozen vegetables or convenience foods. And even in cities where they are available, Mexican women don't trust instant foods and packaged mixes. Instead, they prefer to make everything from scratch. That way they know exactly what is in the food they give to their families.

After all the grinding and measuring, sifting and beating, most Mexican dishes are cooked twice! They are boiled and steamed, or fried and baked, or boiled and roasted. Whatever the combination, many steps go into cooking a Mexican meal.

What families eat at dinner usually depends on

what is available at the local market. Each region is known for its own special foods. Markets in seaside towns, for example, sell lots of fresh fish. Veracruz, a major port on the gulf coast, has many tasty fish dishes. Fried red snapper comes smothered in a tangy tomato sauce.

In the deep seas off the coast of Baja California, fishermen catch batches of turtles. These are used to make a delicious turtle soup, which fills many bowls at mealtime. To the south in Acapulco, it is hot so much of the time that women like to prepare a cold fish salad. They soak sea bass in a sauce of lime juice for a few hours. The citric acid in the juice puffs up the fish so that it almost seems cooked. Chopped into small cubes and mixed with bits of tomato, onion, and spices, it makes a tasty meal on a hot, muggy day.

In the north, where cattle graze and wheat fields sprawl like a patchwork quilt, more beef fills dinner plates, and tortillas are made with flour. In the east coast city of Tampico, cooks top strips of broiled steak with melted cheese. To the west in Jalisco, *pozole*, stewed pork or chicken thickened with hominy, is a favorite dish.

Down in the south, cooks use less hot chile and more black beans. They pickle beef, chicken, and pigs' feet to preserve them in the hot climate, and then roll them up in tortillas to make tacos.

Bananas are popular all over Mexico, but in the south they grow in back yards. They come in all sizes, long and short, fat and thin. There's even a cooking banana called a plantain that Mexicans slice and fry in butter and top with brown sugar and whipped cream.

Today many well-to-do Mexican families eat European-style meals of meat or fish, potatoes or noodles, and a vegetable. In these meals little rolls called *bolillos* take the place of tortillas. Crunchy on the outside, they are soft on the inside, just like our French bread.

Panaderías, where warm rolls are bought fresh from the oven, thrive in even the smallest Mexican towns. In most city neighborhoods, aromas of bread and pastries fill the air. Children call the baker *maestro*, or master, and they like to run errands to the bakery. Regular customers know exactly when the "maestro" bakes and line up as the pastries, cookies, and bolillos are done.

Still, the basic diet of most Mexicans is beans, rice, and corn. In one form or another, these main foods and a big pot of soup are in every kitchen. Out in the countryside, meals are very simple and often meatless. Most families keep a few chickens in their yards, and about once a week they will have one for dinner.

Beans, a good source of protein, are the main part of every meal in many Mexican homes. Often they are cooked on stone hearths in *ollas*, large earthen pots. Most farmers grow enough beans for their family and a little extra to sell at the local market.

In addition to beans, some form of corn is usually served with every meal. Tortillas are made and enjoyed throughout Mexico. A common sound from a Mexican kitchen is the gentle pat-a-pat of the *tortillera*, the tortilla maker. She moistens her hands with a little water and scoops up a small ball of corn *masa*, the dough. Then, with quick, rotating slaps of her palms, she pats out the flat, round tortilla cakes. Little girls practice making tortillas as they watch, but they have to work for years to learn to do it quickly and well.

The modern way to make tortillas is to use a press and stamp them out. And yet, many old tortilleras can turn them out faster than the machines! The art of tortilla making lives on as mothers and grandmothers pass it on to little girls.

Corn masa is also used to make *tamales*. These are favorites for parties and Sunday get-togethers. Making them is a family event in itself, called a *tamalada*.

The mother beats the ground corn with water and shortening, chatting as she works, while her helper mixes the meat filling. Little girls pick out the best dried corn husks and dampen them with water. Big sisters spread the masa on the husk and spoon filling into the middle. Grandmothers know best how to roll the husks around the filling and tie up the ends. Then everyone rests while the tamales steam in a big pot for about an hour.

Each tamale has only a small amount of meat in it. In fact, a little meat can go a long way in Mexican cooking. The meat from one turkey can make as many as 200 tamales. Or, if the meat is shredded, it can be rolled up in tortillas to make just as many tacos.

Tacos are probably the best known Mexican food in the United States and Canada. We think of tacos as a fried tortilla, folded in half and stuffed. But to a Mexican, the word taco means more than just a snack or a light meal. The tortillas can be steamed, fried, rolled, or folded, and almost any food can be used as a filling.

Since tortillas are available in most supermarkets in the United States, you may want to try making yourself a taco snack. Just take a tortilla and place it on a hot griddle or heavy iron skillet over medium-high heat for about thirty seconds, turning it over a few times. Heat up almost any leftover meat—beef, chicken, or pork—sliced into thin strips or shredded.

Put the meat across the middle of the tortilla and add grated cheese, tomato bits, shredded lettuce or alfalfa sprouts, and maybe a dash of mild chile sauce to make it spicy.

Be original with the fillings! Roll one side over the filling and overlap the remaining side to make it like a tube. Then just hold it in your hand like a sandwich and eat it.

Mexicans are used to snacking whenever they are hungry. That's why there are so many little taco stands on the streets of cities and towns. At home Mexican children make tacos for snacks the way we make peanut butter sandwiches.

After all the snacking and the big midday meal, Mexicans aren't too hungry later on in the day. Their evening meals are simple and light, and they are served later than we normally eat dinner. Often they don't even begin until nine o'clock. During this casual and relaxed time, the family catches up on all that happened during the day.

Every member of a Mexican family has an important contribution to make. Earning money, managing the house, learning and growing, loving and caring— all these things help families work together. And being part of a close circle of family and friends makes belonging to a Mexican family something special.

7. *Off to School*

Not too long ago in Mexico, three out of every four people could neither read nor write. Since most schools were in the big cities and towns, country children never went to school. Instead, they were taught how to swing a machete, plant beans, grind corn, and cook.

At last, after the Revolution of 1910, the government began to build schools in remote villages so that many more children could go to school. Today Mexicans spend more money to build schools and buy books than they do on their armed forces. Their country has more teachers than soldiers.

There are still not enough schools for everyone in country areas, but most Mexican children now go to primary school. While they study the same things, no two schools are exactly alike. Some schools have only one room. Others are big and airy, with lots of windows and cheerful colors.

All over the country, in grades one, two, and three, boys and girls learn to read and write, add, subtract, multiply, and divide. They also study some history and science. In the classroom, just as at home, Mexican children respect their elders. They think of

Young people gather for a school assembly at a large secundaria, *similar to a U.S. junior high school.*

their teacher as a guide, someone who will lead them to discovery. In villages the teacher is often more respected than the mayor.

Most Mexican children are grateful to have the chance to go to school. In fact, many Indian boys and girls teach their parents how to read because their parents never learned how. One such little boy is named Pedro. His parents are very proud of him.

Pedro lives near a small village in the mountains of the state of Puebla. The village can only be reached on foot or horseback. Perched on a mesa, it is approached by a narrow footpath that winds up the steep slopes in sharp, hairpin turns. On top the path straightens out and becomes the main road of the village, which is lined with adobe brick, tile-roofed houses. Chickens and dogs run around in yards enclosed by stick fences.

Towards the center of the village, the road is paved with stones, but no cars pass there. Two larger buildings rise up in the main plaza. One is the home of the mayor, who is the oldest son of an ancient Spanish family. The other, which was built only five years ago, is the school.

Pedro, the fourth child of six, lives with his family on a small farm four miles from the village. Though he just had his ninth birthday, he is the oldest child at home now since his brother left for the capital. María, the first daughter, works as a maid for a family in Mexico City. She sends money home to the family each month. Concha married at fifteen and lives with her husband's family nearby. Little brother Luis and baby Ana are still at home.

Because today is a school day, Pedro wakes up at the first light of dawn. He gets up quietly, pulls on his white pants and shirt, and ties them at the waist with a cord. His parents and brother are still sleeping on their straw mats on the dirt floor. His baby sister lies

The land in this picture is much like the rugged, mountainous area where Pedro lives.

bundled up in a cradle which swings gently from the rafters by two thick ropes. His house, like most of the others nearby, is made of sticks with a thatched roof. There are two rooms.

As Pedro comes back from the rain barrel outside, where he splashes water on his face, his mother is busy stoking the coals for cooking. Soon the whole family is up and seated on straight-backed chairs around the brazier, or stone cooking area, in the corner of the bigger room. There is no table in Pedro's house. His mother just fills up some tortillas with beans and hands them out to everyone.

Pedro is excited because he can ride the horse to school today. His father bought the horse with the money María sent from Mexico City. Pedro throws on his serape and straw hat, places the blanket on the horse, and hops on. His mother waves to him from the doorway as he leaves.

Through thickets of coffee plants in the cool upper parts of the hills, down into the rows of corn that follow the curves of the land, Pedro rides along. Everything looks different from horseback. Once in the outskirts of the village, he stops at his uncle's house and ties up the horse under a tree.

Outside the schoolhouse, the children are already lined up waiting to go in. Boys and girls march into the same classroom and sit down at small wooden desks. On the walls are pictures of Mexican heroes— Juárez, Morelos, and Hidalgo. A Mexican flag hangs in the front of the room.

There are fifty-two students in Pedro's class. Just a few years ago, there were one hundred boys and girls in the first grade class. By the end of the year, every child had learned to read and write. The villagers say that Señora Lopez, the teacher, is the best in all of Mexico. Because this year there is a new teacher as well, the classes are smaller.

Pedro is in the class taught by the new teacher, a young woman named Señorita Guzman. His schoolwork begins at nine o'clock when the students take out their homework. Some raise their hands and volunteer to write it on the blackboard. They write words from the list their teacher gave them and correct the spelling.

After reviewing the homework, Señorita Guzman writes the new letter of the alphabet for the day on the board. Then the students practice writing the new letter in their books. They try to think of words that begin with the letter and write them down. Their teacher gives them a sentence to write which uses the new letter as often as possible. Later everyone must write it ten times for homework.

Pedro has had trouble learning the letters and words he needs to know in order to read. He is repeating first grade this year because he didn't pass the government reading test for all first graders. Last year Pedro missed many weeks of school when he had to help his father in the fields. Now, because his little brother Luis can help a little, he is able to attend school more often.

Pedro is working very hard on his reading this year and hopes he will pass the government test. Some girls and boys stay in first grade for three years before they pass the test. None of them can go on to second grade until they do.

After the language lesson comes math. Since

Pedro learned addition and subtraction in the first grade and can do numbers all the way up to one hundred, his teacher gives him work in a second grade book. Right now he is learning multiplication. Señorita Guzman passes up and down the rows while everyone works quietly in their books.

At 12:30 she tells all the children to put their pencils down. It is time for thirty minutes of *descanso*, or recess. Everyone lines up and files outside to play soccer, jump rope, sit and chat, or buy a snack from the nearby taco stand.

Pedro, however, doesn't have time for play. He takes out the tortilla his mother made for him that morning and eats it quickly while he goes over to another teacher, Señor Gomez, to learn about mechanics. Most of the children who live in town spend an hour or two with their teacher each day after the midday meal. During this time they learn crafts and manual jobs. But Pedro cannot return after school because he lives too far away and must leave to help his father.

After descanso the students return to the classroom and spend another thirty minutes finishing their math. Then for the next hour they learn about social science, natural science, music, or art. Yesterday they talked about getting along with other people.

Today they study biology. The teacher sticks a

Like Pedro, this Mexican student spends an hour or two each day learning crafts and manual jobs.

batch of cutout figures —people, animals, snakes, birds, and insects—on the board. The girls and boys must separate all the living things into groups according to how they are born, from eggs or by live-birth. Pedro enjoys this last hour of school.

At two o'clock everyone says goodbye to the teacher and leaves for home. After picking up his horse at his uncle's house, Pedro rides off into the surrounding hills. His father is already home when Pedro arrives.

Soon Pedro's family gathers around the brazier for their main meal of the day—soup, beans, and tortillas. After eating, Pedro and his father lead the horse out to the fields where they plow until sunset.

When they finish their work, the family comes together again for a late supper. Since there is no electricity in Pedro's town, his mother lights a small kerosene lamp. The family usually eats around eight o'clock, and by nine Pedro is ready to lie down on his mat and go to sleep.

Pedro's school is like many others in the rural areas of Mexico. While most boys and girls now finish the sixth grade, only about one out of every four goes on to a higher level. In Pedro's town there is no government *secundaria*, or junior high school. A missionary priest and five nuns started one, but they are still struggling to construct a building.

City schools are bigger. María is a ten-year-old girl in Guadalajara who is in fifth grade in a school near her home. She likes school so much that she wants to be a teacher. María plans to go to secundaria and then to another school for four years to earn her teacher's diploma. If she works very hard in school, she can be a teacher by the time she is nineteen.

María's parents own a small store in a friendly neighborhood. Just behind the store is their Spanish-style house with a cool, shaded patio in the center. María shares one of the three bedrooms with her two sisters.

Every morning María gets up around six o'clock. Taking her clothes from the giant *ropero* against the wall, she dresses quietly so that her sisters will not be awakened. As she walks though the *sala,* or living room, into the kitchen, she can hear the swish of the broom in the store as her mother prepares it to open for business.

In the kitchen Lucrecia, the maid, is preparing eggs, tortillas, and beans on the gas stove. In the corner stands a shiny new washing machine, one of the family's proudest possessions. María sets the table while the rest of the family begins to stir.

For María school starts at eight o'clock. All the girls attend the morning session until noon, and then the boys go to the afternoon session. María says that her teacher is very strict. All thirty-four girls in her class must be silent whenever the teacher speaks, for in her school the teacher slaps and even spanks the children who misbehave.

Today, after language and math, María's class studies geography. The students are learning about the mountains and rivers of Mexico. Just before they

Unlike María's school, this class has girls and boys studying together. A mural has been painted on the back wall of the room.

go home, there is a music lesson. María enjoys music and hopes to study the violin someday.

Right after school, María walks straight home and helps out in the kitchen. Lucrecia is busy cooking dinner while María's mother minds the store. Lucrecia is like an aunt to María, and they chat about school as María sets the table. After the early afternoon dinner, María works in the store and plays with her baby brother.

When the store is closed up for the night, the family eats supper. Later, as they sit comfortably in the sala, María's father talks about his plans to buy a television set soon. María is excited about having a TV at home. As she goes to bed, she says her prayers and imagines what life would be like with a television set.

Not all children in Mexico go to public schools such as those attended by Pedro and María. There are also many private church schools run by priests and nuns. Diego is a student in a private school in Mexico City. His father is the manager of a large company.

Diego's family lives in a modern house in a suburb called Pedregal where lava rocks lie strewn about from a volcanic eruption long, long ago. With eight bedrooms and five baths, it is a big house. Since Diego has twelve brothers and sisters, the house is always full of people. Three of his sisters are married now and live in apartments downtown, but his great-aunt lives with the family, too.

Diego has sandy-brown hair and freckles. His friends call him *güero* because he has fair skin and light hair. Since Diego is twelve years old, he is just starting secundaria. Afterwards he plans to go to preparatory school for three more years, and then on to the university. He says he wants to study medicine or law, perhaps in the United States or Europe. Only about five students out of every hundred go to college in Mexico. Diego must study hard to prepare himself.

As he wakes up on Friday, he is happy because this is the day the whole family leaves for their week-end house in the nearby city of Cuernavaca. That evening, as soon as everyone returns home, they will pack up and ride across the mountains into the sunny valley an hour away.

Since this morning Diego is late as usual, he dresses quickly in his white shirt, blue blazer, and dark pants. He knots his tie as he dashes to the breakfast room and grabs a piece of toast. Chugging a cup of hot chocolate, he runs out to the car where his father is waiting. Because Diego's school is on the way downtown, his father has the driver stop by each day on his way to the office.

As Diego arrives, groups of boys dressed in the same uniform walk quickly up the school steps. Dress codes are very strict in this small private boys' school run by the Roman Catholic order of Dominicans. Some friends wave to Diego as he steps from the long, black car.

With the bell still ringing, Diego slips into his seat. Everyone stands as the Dominican teacher walks into the room and nods good morning to the students. Then the busy day begins—lessons in Spanish, English, French, algebra, history, and chemistry. This year Diego has only one elective, a class he is taking because he likes it and not because it is required. In this class, music, he is learning to play the guitar.

There are no sports or dances at Diego's school, just difficult classes. His teachers are very strict, but they never have to spank or even scold the students. Anyone who does not follow the rules or do his homework is simply told to leave the school.

After school Diego and a few of his friends hail a taxi and go to his family's club. Hamburgers are popular at the club, and the boys order some instead of going home. Since Diego is taking tennis lessons, he is glad to have his friends along to practice with him.

By the time he arrives home, there is only enough time to throw some clothes into a satchel and meet the rest of the family at the car. It's a tight squeeze, but everyone jams into the car and they're off!

Diego always looks forward to weekends in Cuernavaca. The family will get there just in time for supper. Concha, the maid, will have everything on the table for them. She and her husband live there all the time in a little room out back and take care of the house. Diego plans to get a lot of studying done, but he also knows that there will be a big fiesta on Saturday evening at the home of some old family friends. To have fun and study, too, he will have to plan his time well.

Diego is part of the small number of boys, and even smaller one of girls, who study for the university. Each year, though, the numbers are growing. The national university in Mexico City now has more than 110,000 students, and there are many private universities all over Mexico as well.

For many years most Mexicans believed that parents should be responsible for educating their children. But the poor, who could neither read nor write, saw no reason for their own children to go to school. They felt that children were needed more in the fields and at home than in the classroom.

During the past thirty years, this situation has changed a great deal. The government has started huge programs to teach adults how to read and write. Once parents began to learn, they were more willing to let their children go to school.

Today *guarderías*, day-care centers for small children, are popping up all over Mexico. Schools to teach mechanics, metalworking, and many other trades are filled with students who have no more than a sixth-grade education. Factories run huge training programs for workers and special schools for their children. Many small, private schools teach typing and computer skills. And everywhere, Mexicans want to learn English.

Mexicans see schooling as a way to improve their lives through training for better jobs. When all their people have the opportunity to get a good education, another great step will have been made in the growth of the nation.

8. Bullfights in the Afternoon

Of all the sports in Mexico, the *corrida de toros*, or bullfight, is the most exciting and dramatic. Everywhere in Mexico, little boys practice fancy passes with imaginary bulls. Even the tiniest town has a place for bullfights. Larger towns have special places for the corrida such as a fenced-in arena and some bleachers. But the biggest bullring in all the world, the Plaza de Toros Monumental, is in Mexico City.

Mexico's bullfight fans, called *aficionados*, flock to the plaza every Sunday afternoon at four o'clock to watch their favorite *matador*. Thousands of spectators fill the stands from late October until March during the big season. Then the off season begins, featuring younger and less well known matadors who fight young bulls. There's always a bullfight somewhere on a Sunday afternoon.

Bullfighting is an important part of Mexican culture. The tradition is an old one which was brought to Mexico by the Spaniards. In fact, the first bullfight held in Mexico was in 1529, only eight years after the Spanish conquest.

The corrida has all the excitement of a theater play and the grace of a ballet, but above all, the

matador must show his courage. It starts with a colorful opening parade of the bullfighters who will face
the bulls in the ring. A horseman leads the marchers
in a great circle around the arena. As the parade
moves along its way, a band plays the beat of a Latin
American march step, the *paso-doble*.

Usually there are three matadors, who wear
richly embroidered short jackets, tight fitting knee
pants, and stockings. These suits are known as *trajes
de luces*, "suits of light," because they glitter and
sparkle so much. The matadors wear their hair
twisted into a knot, with a single, thin lock of hair on
the nape of the neck. On top of their heads sits a flat
hat with pointed corners.

Each matador has helpers. First come the *banderilleros*, wearing similar, but less bright costumes.
Next come the *picadores*, dressed in thick leather
trousers and a flat-brimmed hat. Finally, in the rear
of the parade, are the group of attendants and a team
of mules that will drag off the dead bull.

After the parade has circled the arena, the horseman dashes over to where the *presidente* of the plaza
is seated. He salutes the public officials and asks their
permission to begin the bullfight. Then, as the
marchers follow the horseman out of the ring, the
music quiets, and the crowd hushes to a whisper.

When all is silent, the presidente waves to signal

*Dressed in his "suit of light," a matador marches proudly into
the Plaza de Toros Monumental in Mexico City.*

the opening of the gate to let in the first bull. Up in the stands, thousands of fans cheer and trumpets blast as the bull thunders out of the gate, snorts, and paws the ground.

At last the bullfight begins. First, the banderilleros run out to test the bull. When they wave their capes, the bull charges. The matador stays behind a wooden gate where he can study the bull. He watches how the bull hooks with his horns and how it attacks and turns. In this way he gets to know it a little before meeting it face-to-face. Then, when he is ready, the matador comes out and waves his bright pink working cape lined with gold satin. He teases the bull and tests its speed.

Next the picadors have their turn. On horseback, with the horses protected by thick pads on their flanks and chests, the picadors gallop past the bull. As they pass it, they prick the wide part of its neck with long lances. This wound cuts certain muscles and makes the bull's head hang lower. The picadors must hit the bull at least three times. All the while, the crowd boos and jeers at them, but they ignore the yelling.

Sometimes the picador's horse is pushed over by a bull. Then the matador rushes out and attracts the bull's attention away from the horse with some sweeping passes of his bright cape. The crowd always feels sorry for the horse, but no one worries about the picadors. Tradition holds that they should be insulted, not cheered.

After the picadors comes the placing of the *banderillas* in the hump on the bull's neck. Three pairs of banderillas, arrowlike sticks with a sharp, barbed end, must pierce the muscles in the neck. The banderilleros run at the bull and stick the barbs into the neck so that only the dangling ribbons show. These wounds lower the bull's head even more and make it madder than ever.

As trumpets blast, the last part of the bullfight begins. Now the matador meets the bull alone. First, he exchanges the working cape of pink and gold for a smaller, red cape, the *muleta*. Sometimes the matador steps up to the presidente and announces that he wishes to dedicate the bull to a special person among the spectators. According to tradition, though, he must first offer it to the presidente.

Since the matador has studied the bull, he knows exactly what kind of passes will work best. He teases the bull and calls out to it, "*aïe, toro*." He may drag the muleta along the ground as the bull follows it with his horns, or he may pass the muleta right over the bull's horns as the bull tries to hook it.

Sometimes the bull comes so close to the matador that he tears his clothing. Once in a while, a matador is gored by a bull. But in the most beautiful bullfights,

Leading with his muleta, *a matador draws the bull in a flowing circle around him.*

the matador shows that he has complete control over the bull. He makes one smooth, flowing pass that leads the bull in a great circle around him as the bull follows the muleta. The bull charges after it, snorting and hooking.

After he has worked the bull with a series of passes and shown his courage in the face of this huge, angry creature, the matador is ready for the kill. The entire plaza quiets down to a whisper. All eyes are fixed on the matador as he pulls the short sword out from the muleta. Before he can attempt a kill, he must have calmed the bull so that it is standing still.

The matador holds the sword and looks the bull right in the eye. Sometimes the bull charges the matador and lunges right into the sword. At other times the matador attacks the bull and thrusts the sword. When he has placed the sword well, the bull falls dead at the matador's feet.

As the crowd cheers, a team of mules trots in to drag the dead bull out of the arena. Meanwhile, the matador walks in a circle around the ring to receive the crowd's applause. When he has fought very, very well, aficionados wave white handkerchiefs in the air. Then the presidente makes a sign that the matador should get a prize. An ear is cut off the bull, and the matador takes another turn around the ring, holding it up for everyone to see. Admirers throw flowers and hats to him, and some even throw their jackets and sweaters. Bullfighters are great heroes in Mexico.

While all Mexicans enjoy bullfights, few become famous matadors. But there are many other ways for Mexicans to spend their time in active sports.

Horseback riding has been popular ever since the Spaniards brought the first horses to Mexico. Today there are hundreds of riding groups all over the country. Called *charro* clubs, these groups are especially popular in the cattle country of the northwestern plains.

Charreadas, which are much like rodeos north of the Rio Grande, are held on Sunday mornings in many small towns and in Guadalajara. In fact, rodeos as we know them in the United States and Canada came from Mexico through Texas and the Southwest. The word *rodeo* is a Spanish word meaning "roundup."

The first recorded rodeo in Mexico took place in 1538 when *vaqueros*, or cowboys, rounded up the grazing cattle. The word *buckaroo* is really *vaquero* pronounced in an American way. Many other cowboy words we use today come from Mexico. The lariat was *la reata*, the lasso comes from *lazo*, and chaps are short for *chaparreras*.

If Mexico has a national team sport, it is *fútbol*, which is pronounced like the American *football* but means "soccer." Long ago the Mayas and Aztecs played *Pok-to-Pok*, a game somewhat like modern soccer. Today Mexicans follow their favorite teams in the sports pages of the newspapers, and huge crowds flock to playoff games and international championships. During a big game, business comes to a halt, and any man on the street can tell you the current score.

For most important games in Mexico City, the big stadium is filled with noisy fans well before game time. The stadium can hold more than 100,000 screaming fans and has more than 700 private boxes. Some of the boxes are fitted with bathrooms and telephones and come with their own numbered parking spaces. During a game the fans cheer and yell for their team. When they are unhappy about a play, they whistle rather than boo.

The best soccer players quickly become national heroes, and all over Mexico little boys dream of becoming famous like them. Mexican boys play soccer anytime and anywhere they can—in country school yards, empty lots, and city streets. Millions of them enjoy the excitement of the game.

While bullfighting, charreadas, and soccer have long been popular in Mexico, in recent years Mexicans have shown an interest in other sports. Much of this new interest began during the 1968 summer Olympic Games in Mexico City. When athletes first arrived there for the games, they had to adjust to the high altitude and thin air. Some went to the capital weeks in advance to get used to the climate so that they could perform at their best. Despite the high altitude problems, the games went well and sparked Mexicans' interest in many new sports.

New words such as *gimnasia* ("gymnastics"), *boxeo* ("boxing"), *lucha libre* ("wrestling"), and *salto de altura* ("high jumping") popped into everyday speech. *Ciclismo* ("cycling") and *esquí* ("skiing"), are now becoming popular sports. The latest fad among many Mexico City residents is *trote corto*, or jogging.

Baseball, golf, and tennis are big sports in Mexico, too. Mexican baseball players now play for such U.S. teams as the San Diego Padres and Los Angeles Dodgers. Tennis players often place in the top ten in international matches. And in many parts of the country, private clubs sell memberships for use of their tennis courts and golf courses.

While few Mexicans can afford to buy club memberships, some sports are free. Since no one can own the beaches in Mexico, anyone can swim. And along its more than five thousand miles of coastline, Mexico has many fine beaches.

Another water sport, sailing, is popular along the coasts and in the lakes of Mexico. Sailing races, called regattas, are held at different times of the year in Acapulco, Cancún, and Manzanillo. Smaller regattas take place in Lake Pátzcuaro and Lake Avándaro high in the mountains about an hour and a half from Mexico City.

Imagine what it would be like to take a ride on the scary "Russian Mountain" in Chapultepec Park.

Unlike many sports and games in Mexico, amusement parks are more fun for children than adults. Chapultepec Park in Mexico City has one of the best in the world. The Russian Mountain, one of the scariest roller coaster rides anywhere, towers over the trees and lakes of this large and beautiful park.

Zoos are places for Mexican children to have fun, too. In Puebla families take a drive through Safari Land where they can watch lions, tigers, elephants, and hippopotamuses through the windows of their cars. All the animals roam about freely, while the people stay safely inside.

If Mexican children can't visit the zoos or the amusement parks, they can see the circus when it comes to town. There are big, three-ring circuses in the cities and smaller, one-ring circuses in little towns. Children eat peanuts and snacks as they watch the lion tamer and acrobats and laugh at the funny faces of the clowns. Everyone likes the circus!

From bullfights to circuses, soccer matches to charreadas, and sailing to baseball, Mexicans take part in many sports and kinds of recreation. The ancient sports are full of tradition, while many others are brand new. Some Mexicans like to watch, and many others prefer to play. Whatever kind of sports or recreation they enjoy, in Mexico they can find it.

9. At Home in the United States

When Americans first study the history of the United States, they learn about the thirteen colonies begun by English settlers in the East. But long before the Pilgrims landed in New England, Spanish explorers had pushed their way slowly into the deserts and mountains of the Southwest. Almost one-fourth of what is now the United States was once part of New Spain and Mexico. In fact, the story of the Mexican people and the people of Texas, New Mexico, Arizona, and California were one for many years.

In the 1500s Spanish explorers set off from Mexico to look for riches in the American Southwest. Soon missionaries moved in to bring Christianity to the Indians and settle the lands. By 1580 churches were established in Indian villages. In the late 1590s, a settlement stood in Santa Fe, now the capital of New Mexico. Will Rogers, famous American humorist, once joked that when Captain John Smith landed in Virginia to begin the first English colony, New Mexicans could have sent a group to welcome him.

Before long Spanish explorers traveled up the western coast to a land they named California. By 1697 fifteen missions stretched along nine hundred miles of land from Baja to Alta California. But few white settlers went to this distant land because the Indians there attacked the white invaders. The missions struggled. Then, as Russian settlements moved to within fifty miles of San Francisco, efforts began to send colonists from Mexico to defend the colony.

In Mexico City plans were drawn up to build permanent towns in Alta California. The goal was to set the missions one day's journey on foot apart on a road which was called "El Camino Real."

Franciscan missionaries from Mexico City were sent to replace the Jesuits who had built the early missions. The Franciscans built a church, sleeping quarters, and workrooms around a central courtyard at each site. This part was the mission. To protect it from Indians, soldiers were stationed at the nearby *presidio*, or military headquarters.

Fray Junípero Serra is perhaps the best known Franciscan missionary of this period. In fifteen years of service, he helped carry out a settlement plan called the "Sacred Expedition." The first ship, the *San Antonio*, set sail from Baja California and landed in San Diego on April 11, 1769. Father Serra's group, arriving shortly afterwards on foot and mule, founded the first missions at Old Town in San Diego.

Soon engineers, muleteers, and twenty-seven soldiers left the settlement to locate sites for the other

N

CALIFORNIA MISSIONS

SAN FRANCISCO SOLANO de SONOMA

SAN RAFAEL ARCANGEL

SAN JOSE de GUADALUPE

SAN FRANCISCO de ASIS

SANTA CLARA de ASIS

SANTA CRUZ

SAN JUAN BAUTISTA

SAN CARLOS de RIO CARMEL

NUESTRA SENORA de la SOLEDAD

SAN ANTONIO de PADUA

SAN MIGUEL ARCANGEL

SAN LUIS OBISPO de TOLOSA

LA PURISIMA CONCEPTION

SANTA INEZ

SAN FERNANDO REY

SANTA BARBARA

SAN BUENAVENTURA

SAN GABRIEL

SAN JUAN CAPISTRANO

SAN LUIS REY de FRANCIA

SAN DIEGO de ALCALA

missions. At each site the Spanish governor planted the royal standard, uprooted plants, and cast stones to the four winds. This ceremony meant that he was seizing the land for the king of Spain.

The first large group of emigrants from Mexico, 240 colonists from Sonora, left for San Francisco in September 1775. They reached the new mission almost six months later with 165 mules, 304 horses, and 302 cattle. One person died, but eight babies were born during the trip.

After ten years each mission became a town, and all the Indians who worked there, citizens. The mission kept only the church and the living quarters for the parish priest. The other buildings became public buildings for services to the people. All the crops and herds then belonged to the whole town, which was governed by a commissioner.

Life was peaceful in the northern territories of New Spain. Old Spanish families held huge ranches that spread for miles and miles, and the missions grew and prospered. By 1820, however, the rumblings of the independence movement had spread to the edges of the empire. Then, when Mexico won independence from Spain in 1821, all the land became part of the Republic of Mexico.

In the years following independence from Spain, Mexico welcomed settlers from the United States

Today visitors come to see the restored mission of San Juan Capistrano between Los Angeles and San Diego.

into California and the northern part of Coahuila, now the state of Texas. They gave the Americans land to farm.

The newcomers brought strong ideas of independence with them. In 1836 the Americans and the Mexicans joined together to revolt against Mexico and set up the new Lone Star Republic of Texas. Ten years later and far to the west, some old Spanish families, called *Californios*, joined with the newcomers to declare the Bear Flag Republic of California.

War had already broken out one month earlier between Mexico and the United States. When U.S. troops marched into Mexico City, the fighting ended with the signing of the Treaty of Guadalupe. The United States took over all the land north of the Rio Grande. New Mexico, California, Nevada, most of Arizona, and part of Colorado were turned over to the United States in exchange for 15 million dollars. More than one-half of the Mexican empire became part of the United States.

This was the turning point in U.S.-Mexican history. Mexicans no longer ruled the northern lands. Then, with the discovery of gold, thousands of people flooded into California. Caravans of covered wagons careened across the prairies, and ships sailed around Cape Horn to San Francisco. Like the Spanish explorers three hundred years earlier, they followed the dream of gold and quick riches.

As the newcomers arrived with their own laws and customs, the old Spanish-Mexican ways disappeared. Soon there were more Americans than Mexicans. One year after California became a state, the U.S. Congress passed the Land Act of 1851 to require the inspection of all land titles. Within a few years, almost all of the land owned by the Californios was lost to newcomers, and many Mexicans fled from their homes across the new border to the south. Other laws banned foreigners from the gold mines and from owning land.

Meanwhile, in Arizona, Mexicans and Americans fought side by side against a common enemy, the Apaches. While many Mexicans worked in the mines and tilled the fields, Americans controlled Arizona's businesses and its politics. In the 1870s, when copper, gold, and silver were discovered in Arizona, adventurers, wild men, and some serious settlers rushed in. Just as in California, Mexicans soon found themselves far outnumbered.

In Texas the scars of the war with Mexico were lasting and deep. Most of the small Mexican population centered around the border in the south. The Americans lived in the central and northern areas. Both remained separate and proud of their way of life.

New Mexico, on the other hand, had a large Mexican population. When newcomers arrived, they found it difficult to break up the old sheep and cattle ranches. Towns, also, were organized and strong. Santa Fe was a major trading center. In New Mexico more than in any other part of the Southwest, Mexicans were involved in public life. When the state constitution was written in 1911, full and equal rights were granted to the Spanish-speaking people. The two cultures and the two languages were accepted all over the state.

Since the early days of settlements in the American Southwest, millions of Mexicans have come to the United States. Many fled to the north because the battles of the Revolution of 1910 made life difficult. Business was slow in Mexico, and roaming soldiers made farming impossible.

Then, when the United States entered World War I in 1917, American businesses needed men and women to work in factories. Farmers needed help to plant and harvest the fields. To attract workers, the U.S. government invited Mexicans to move to the United States. Many came legally, with papers, while still more crossed the border illegally. All came in search of work.

During the boom years of the 1920s, nearly half a million Mexicans came to America looking for work.

Most were poor farmers who had no skills, but some doctors, lawyers, and other skilled professionals came, too. In fact, so many Mexicans immigrated to the United States that Mexican government officials became alarmed.

Beginning in 1929, the Great Depression changed everything. As more and more Americans lost their jobs and work was hard to find, fewer Mexicans crossed the border. With millions of Americans out of work, government officials began to send Mexican Americans back to Mexico. They were given train fare for the trip. Thousands of people who could not prove that they had entered the country legally were sent across the border. Even some who were born in the United States were sent to Mexico with their immigrant parents.

After the United States entered World War II in 1941, U.S. businesses needed workers once more. Congress passed a law that allowed Mexican workers to cross the border to work for a short time. Called *braceros*, these day laborers could not stay, and they had to return to Mexico when the work season ended. Since the workers were not citizens, they never earned as much as Americans. They were happy to get work, though, for even the lowest paying job in the United States paid more than they could earn in Mexico.

While the bracero program officially ended in

1964, Mexican workers continue to follow the harvests throughout the Southwest and as far north as Michigan, Minnesota, Idaho, and Washington. There is now a limit to the number of new immigrants who may come to the United States each year. Still, any Mexican who has a relative in the United States is allowed to come. Thousands still immigrate each year in search of better jobs with higher pay.

In addition to those who come legally, many Mexicans cross over the border each day illegally in search of work. They brave deserts and climb over rugged mountains at night to slip past the border patrol. The illegal Mexicans are known as "wetbacks" because they sometimes swim or wade across the Rio Grande.

Though much of the two-thousand-mile border is barren desert, most illegal crossings take place near cities such as El Paso and San Diego. Smugglers arrange for workers to get jobs and carry them across the border in trucks and jeeps or even stuffed into the trunks of cars. Called "coyotes," the smugglers charge from two to three hundred dollars or more for the trip.

Officers of the U.S. border patrol say that the only way to fully stop the illegal crossings would be to post guards every twenty feet along the entire border. That would require more than half a million guards!

Both the illegal Mexicans and the border police consider the crossings mostly a game. Even when the illegals are caught and sent across the border to Mexico, they just wait a few minutes and sneak right back over.

Many employers hire illegals because they can pay them low wages without any social security and benefits. Homemakers in El Paso, Houston, Los Angeles, San Diego, and many other cities cheer when their maids make it back across the border. They pay them only about twenty-five dollars a week and could never afford to hire a maid if they had to pay legal minimum wages.

A new bill was passed by Congress in 1982 to try to stop the flow of illegal aliens into the United States. As a result, employers who are found to have illegal workers in their shop, farm, or house will have to pay a fine.

Many American businesses avoid the problem of hiring illegal Mexicans by building factories just on the other side of the border. To date, 620 of these factories, called *maquiladoras*, stretch from the Gulf of Mexico to the Pacific coast. Thousands of Mexicans sew blue jeans, assemble electronic parts, and make dolls. Four out of five of these workers are women who earn the Mexican minimum wage of 280 pesos, or about four U.S. dollars, for an eight-hour day.

New Mexican immigrants to the United States tend to move into neighborhoods known as *barrios* where many other Mexican Americans live. In the barrio everyone speaks Spanish, and most people follow traditional Mexican ways. From the neat rows of little houses in East Los Angeles to the tin-roofed shacks along highways on the west side of San Antonio, children are raised speaking Spanish at home.

Because Mexican-American children grow up speaking Spanish, providing a good education for them in English-speaking schools has been a problem. In some areas bilingual education is used. The teacher speaks to all the children in English, but the children can write and read books in Spanish. In other areas educators insist that all children must learn English, and only English, in school.

Whatever the method, there is a large and growing need for educating Spanish-speaking children. Today the Mexican-American population in the United States may be as high as eight million. With a high birth rate and steady immigration from Mexico, their numbers are increasing every day. Some reports say that more than half of all Californians will be Mexican Americans within the next twenty years.

Along with their growing numbers, Mexican Americans have shown new interest in studying their roots. In fact, many now call themselves *chicanos* instead of Mexican Americans. Chicano studies programs are offered in many colleges and universities throughout the United States.

Oregon has a school named after the well-known Chicano union organizer, César Chavez. Born and raised on a farm in Yuma, Arizona, Chavez went with his family to California where they became migrant farm workers. He understands the problems of the migrant workers and struggles for fair wages and legal protections for them in the United States.

In cities with many Mexican-Americans, Chicano political groups have grown powerful. Such names as Trujillo, Ramírez, and García appear in local town councils, state boards and legislatures, and the U.S. Congress. In 1981 the citizens of San Antonio elected Dr. Henry Cisneros mayor after he served for six years on the city council. He also holds a position on the faculty of the University of Texas at San Antonio and has been listed three times in *Outstanding Young Men of America.*

Dr. Henry Cisneros,
San Antonio mayor.

Lee Trevino, one of golf's finest players.

Mexican Americans have made their mark in sports, too. Danny Villanueva was a star football player for the Los Angeles Rams and later played with the Dallas Cowboys. Pancho Gonzalez still ranks among the best tennis players of the world. Lee

Trevino, now a sportscaster, was one of golf's finest players, and Nancy Lopez has won many tournaments in women's golf. Major league baseball teams have many top players with Mexican names such as Morales, Hernandez, Guerrero, and Orosco. Often compared to Babe Ruth, Fernando Valenzuela of the Los Angeles Dodgers is one of baseball's best pitchers. We can even see his smiling face on boxes of corn flakes!

Fernando Valenzuela of the Los Angeles Dodgers has won the Cy Young Award as the National League's best pitcher.

Music lovers enjoy the singing of Trini López. Television viewers all over the country watch Eric Estrada play "Panch" on "CHIPS."

Today, then, Mexican Americans play an active role in American life, from government to education to entertainment. The great-great-great grandchildren of the Spanish settlers and American Indians still live in places named by their forefathers— California, Texas, Nevada, Arizona, New Mexico, Colorado, and Montana. From El Paso to San Francisco, cities, rivers, and mountains have Spanish names.

Everywhere in the American Southwest, Mexican roots run deep—in the restored missions, the Spanish-style ranch homes, the barrios, and the taco restaurants. When Mexicans cross over the border, many of them don't feel that they are moving into a foreign land. For in a way, they are coming home.

Appendix A

Mexican Consulates in the United States and Canada

The Mexican consulates in the United States and Canada want to help Americans and Canadians understand Mexican ways. For information and resource materials about Mexico, contact the consulate or embassy nearest you.

U. S. Consulates

Chicago, Illinois
Consulate General of Mexico
201 N. Wells Street
26th Floor
Chicago, Illinois 60606
Phone (312) 372-6190

Dallas, Texas
Consulate General of Mexico
4229 N. Central Expressway
Dallas, Texas 75205
Phone (214) 522-9740

El Paso, Texas
Consulate General of Mexico
Continental Bank Building
601 N. Mesa
El Paso, Texas 79901

Los Angeles, California
Consulate General of Mexico
125 Paseo Plaza
Los Angeles, California 90012
Phone (213) 624-3261

New Orleans, Louisiana
Consulate General of Mexico
1140 International Trade Mart
2 Canal Street
New Orleans, Louisiana 70130

New York, New York
Consulate General of Mexico
8 E. 41st Street
New York, New York 10017
Phone (212) 689-0456

San Antonio, Texas
Consulate General of Mexico
127 Navarro Street
San Antonio, Texas 78205
Phone (512) 227-9145

San Francisco, California
Consulate General of Mexico
870 Market Street
Suite 516
San Francisco, California 94102
Phone (415) 392-5554

Washington, D.C.
Embassy of Mexico
2829 16th Street N.W.
Washington, D.C. 20009
Phone (202) 234-6000

Canadian Consulates

Montreal, Quebec
    Consulate General of Mexico
    1000 Sherbrooke Street West
    Suite 2170
    Montreal, Quebec H3A 2P3
    Phone (514) 288-2502
Ottawa, Ontario
    Embassy of Mexico
    130 Albert Street
    Suite 206
    Ottawa, Ontario K1P 5G4
    Phone (613) 233-8988
Toronto, Ontario
    Consulate General of Mexico
    60 Bloor Street West
    Suite 203
    Toronto, Ontario M4W 3B8
    Phone (416) 922-2718
Vancouver, British Columbia
    Consulate General of Mexico
    310-625 Howe Street
    Vancouver, British Columbia V6C 2T6
    Phone (604) 684-3547

Glossary

abrazo—a hug or embrace

aficionados—fans, usually of sports

angelitos—"little angels"; babies

banderillas—a small dart with a streamer hanging from the blunt end, used by banderilleros to wound a bill

banderilleros—the men who thrust the banderillas into the bull

barrios—a neighborhood or district in a city; the areas in American cities where most Mexican Americans live

bolillos—small rolls or buns

boxeo—boxing

braceros—day laborers; braceros were encouraged to work in the United States by a U.S. government program that ended in 1964

Californios—"Californians"; usually refers to the early Spanish settlers in California

campesino—Mexican peasant, a farmer or farm-worker

chaparreras—leather coverings to protect legs from brambles while horseback riding

charreadas—events similar to American rodeos that feature skilled riders

charro—a horseman; (**charra**—a horsewoman)

chayote—a pear-shaped fruit

chicano—a Mexican American

chicharrones—cracklings; pork fat fried until crispy

chile en nogada—a holiday dish of chili peppers in a white sauce topped with pomegranate seeds

chinampas—small gardens built on reed frames which float in shallow water; the Aztecs used chinampas to grow vegetables on the shallow waters of Lake Texcoco surrounding Tenochtitlán

china poblana—the Mexican national dress for women and girls

ciclismo—cycling

corrida de toros—bullfight

corridos—romantic folk songs that tells the tales of Mexican heroes

criollos—Creoles; persons of Spanish ancestry who were born in New Spain

descanso—a rest, nap, or quiet time

dulces—sweets, candies, and candied fruit

ejidos—public lands which are used and controlled by the people of a village

encomiendas—large estates granted by Spanish kings

esquí—skiing

federales—Mexican government police or soldiers

fiesta—a party, celebration, festival, or holiday

fotonovelas—short romances told through pictures with words written in

fútbol—soccer

gimnasia—gymnastics

grito—a cry or shout

guardería—a day-care center for preschool children

güero—a blond or fair-haired person

haciendas—large farms, ranches, or plantations

huaraches—sandals woven of strips of leather, often made out of old tires cut into soles

huevos—eggs

huevos rancheros—fried eggs served on a warm tortilla and topped with hot chili sauce

jarabe tapatío—the Mexican hat dance

jícama—a root vegetable

kiosque—a small pavilion, refreshment stand, or newsstand

lazo—a loop or lasso

leche—milk

lucha-libre—wrestling

machismo—a strongly masculine attitude and behavior; extreme manliness

maestro—a teacher or master

maquiladoras—U.S.-owned factories along the Mexican side of the border where goods are assembled by Mexican workers

mariachi—street bands for hire to play at parties and other events

marimba—a kind of xylophone with wooden plates of different sizes and gourds or metal tubes underneath the plates as resonators; the marimba is played with rubber or felt-tipped mallets

masa—dough; corn masa is used to make tortillas

matador—a skilled bullfighter who kills the bull

mestizo—a person of Spanish and Indian ancestry

muleta—a bullfighter's red cloth, draped over a rod, which is used to challenge the bull

nacimiento—"birth"; during the Christmas season in Mexico, *nacimiento* means a nativity scene

Náhuatl—the language of the Aztecs

ollas—round earthen pots, or wide-mouthed jars

panadería—bakery

pan de muerto—sweet bread with nuts and raisins, which is shaped like bones to celebrate All Soul's Day, November 1

paseo—a walk, a drive, or an outing; a get-together in the town plaza for young men and women

paso-doble—A Latin American march step often played at bullfights

pelado—a person from the poor end of town

peninsulares—Spaniards in New Spain

peso—the basic unit of money in Mexico

picador—in a bullfight, a horseman armed with a spear who goads the bull

piñata—an animal-shaped, papier-mâché container filled with sweets which is broken open with sticks by a blindfolded person at Mexican parties

piropos—flattering remarks; compliments

posada—a lodging or inn; on the nine nights before Christmas, a procession in memory of the search for an inn by Mary and Joseph

pozole—a common dish made of boiled barley or hominy, beans, and meat

presidente—the president

presidio—a garrison or military headquarters

reata—any rope, but especially a lariat used to tie horses

rebozo—a woman's shawl

ropero—a wardrobe, a large, free-standing wooden closet

Rosca de los Reyes—a twisted ring cake served on January 6, the traditional day for gift giving in Mexico

rurales—in times past, a rural police force used by Mexican governments to keep order

sala—a living room or other large room in a house

salto de altura—the high jump

secundaria—a secondary school similar to a junior high school in the United States

señora—a married woman

señorita—a young, unmarried woman

serape—a narrow blanket worn by men

taco—red meat or chicken, shredded cheese, chopped lettuce, tomato, and onion rolled up in a soft tortilla or in a fried, folded tortilla

tamalada—a gathering to make tamales

tamales—a soft corn meal, stuffed with meat, rolled up in corn husks, and steamed

tapatío—a person or thing from Guadalajara; also used to mean the *jarabe tapatío*, or Mexican hat dance

telenovelas—TV shows similar to American soap operas, but only aired once a week

tierra caliente—the hotlands or tropics

tilma—a cloak fastened at the shoulder by a knot

tortillas—flat, round cakes made of corn meal

tortillera—a person who makes tortillas

trajes de luces—"suits of light," worn by bullfighters, and decorated with sparkling braid and fringe

trote corto—jogging

vaqueros—cowboys

Selected Bibliography

Books for Younger Readers

Amescua, Carol Connor. *The Story of Pablo, Mexican Boy*. New York: Britannica Books, Meredith Press, 1962.

Beck, Barbara L. *The First Book of the Ancient Maya*. New York: Franklin Watts, 1965.

Benitez, Fernando. *In the Footsteps of Cortes*. New York: Pantheon Books, 1952.

Buehr, Walter. *The Spanish Conquistadores in North America*. New York: G. P. Putnam's Sons, 1962.

Calderon de la Barca, Frances E. *Life in Mexico*. New York: E. P. Dutton, 1913.

Coy, Harold. *Chicago Roots Go Deep*. Binghamton, New York: Vail-Ballou Press, 1975.

Credle, Ellis. *Mexico, Land of Hidden Treasure*. Camden, New Jersey: Nelson and Sons, 1967.

Farquhar, Margaret C. *The Indians of Mexico*. New York: Holt, Rinehart, and Winston, 1967.

Geis, Darlene. *Let's Travel in Mexico*. Chicago: Children's Press, 1965.

Larralde, Elsa. *The Land and People of Mexico*. Philadelphia: J. B. Lippincott, 1964.

McNeer, May. *The Mexican Story*. New York: Ariel Books, 1953.

Nava, Julian. *Mexican Americans Past, Present, and Future*. Sacramento: California State Series, 1973.

Nolen, Barbara. *Mexico Is People: Land of Three Cultures*. New York: Scribner's, 1973.

Pinchot, Jane. *The Mexicans in America*. Minneapolis: Lerner, 1973.

Pine, Tillie S., and Levine, Joseph. *The Mayans Knew*. New York: McGraw-Hill, 1971.

Price, Christine. *Heirs of Ancient Maya: The Lacandon Indians of Mexico*. New York: Scribner's, 1972.

Rohmer, Harriet, and Anchondo, Mary. *How We Came to the Fifth World/Como Vinimos al Quinto Mundo*. San Francisco: Children's Book Press, 1976.

Sherrod, Jane, and Singer, Kurt. *Folk Tales of Mexico*. Minneapolis: Denison, 1969.

Von Hagen, Victor W. *The Sun Kingdom of the Aztecs*. Cleveland: The World Publishing Company, 1958.

Index

About the Author

Eileen Latell Smith's wide-ranging international experiences have given her an exceptional insight into the culture and the people of several nations. She went to Mexico as a lay missionary and lived and taught at a remote Mexican village. Later she studied and taught at the Instituto de Relaciones Culturales in Mexico City.

During a two-year stay in Brazil, Ms. Smith taught at the USIS Bi-National Center in São Paulo, and she studied and worked in France in Grenoble, Lyon, and rural Limonest. While residing in Tokyo for four years, she taught English to more than one million students through her appearances on Japanese educational television. In Japan she also collaborated on the writing of a textbook and a series of picture books for young people.

A native New Yorker, the author was educated at Georgetown University, the Université de Grenoble, Columbia University, and the University of California. She now lives with her husband and two daughters on a cattle ranch in northern California and is a lecturer in French and Spanish at California State University.